Methods Beyo
Interviewing in Qualitativ
Market Research

3
QMR

QUALITATIVE MARKET RESEARCH

The seven volumes of *Qualitative Market Research: Principle and Practice* provide complete coverage of qualitative market research practice. It offers commercial practitioners authoritative source texts for training and professional development, and provides academic students and researchers an account of qualitative research theory and practice in use today. Each book cross-references others in the series, but can also be used as a stand-alone resource on a key topic.

❶ *An Introduction to Qualitative Market Research*
Mike Imms and Gill Ereaut

❷ *Interviewing Groups and Individuals in Qualitative Market Research*
Joanna Chrzanowska

❸ *Methods Beyond Interviewing in Qualitative Market Research*
Philly Desai

❹ *Analysis and Interpretation in Qualitative Market Research*
Gill Ereaut

❺ *Developing Brands with Qualitative Market Research*
Jon Chandler and Mike Owen

❻ *Developing Advertising with Qualitative Market Research*
Judith Wardle

❼ *Delivering Results in Qualitative Market Research*
Geraldine Lillis

Gill Ereaut has worked in qualitative market research in the UK for more than 20 years. She now combines teaching and writing on qualitative research with commercial research practice.

With 25 years' industry experience, **Mike Imms** has worked extensively for the Association for Qualitative Research and is a Fellow of Market Research Society. He runs a training organisation for commercial qualitative researchers.

Martin Callingham was Group Market Research Director, Whitbread PLC and is now a consultant. He is a Visiting Professor at Birkbeck College, London University and a Fellow of the Market Research Society.

Methods Beyond Interviewing in Qualitative Market Research

3

QMR

Philly Desai

SAGE Publications
London • Thousand Oaks • New Delhi

SAGE Publications Ltd
6 Bonhill Street
London EC2A 4PU

SAGE Publications Inc.
2455 Teller Road
Thousand Oaks, California 91320

SAGE Publications India Pvt Ltd
32, M-Block Market
Greater Kailash - I
New Delhi 110 048

British Library Cataloguing in Publication data

A catalogue record for this book is available
from the British Library

ISBN 0 7619 7272 2

Library of Congress Control Number 2002101993

Typeset by SIVA Math Setters, Chennai, India
Printed in Great Britain by Antony Rowe, Chippenham, Wiltshire

Contents

Acknowledgements

The following very generously shared their experiences and expertise during the research for this project:

Martin Bontoft, Darryl Burchell, Rachel Carter, Robin Clarke, Barbie Clarke, Sharon DiMoldenberg, Steven Donaldson, Mark Earls, David Farrow, Trazie Flynn, Kirsty Fuller, Neil Goodlad, Kathryn Hall, Bill Parton, Bill Pegram, Christine Roberts, John Rodgers, Guy Rubin, Siamack Salari, Roger Sykes, Helen Trevaskis, Scott Lee, Vanessa Tippet and Debbie Whitehead.

Mike Imms and Gill Ereaut provided valuable editorial guidance and unflagging enthusiasm.

Nick Long, Hy Mariampolski and Sue Robson read the first draft of the manuscript and made many helpful comments.

Editorial Introduction

About Qualitative Market Research:
A Background to the Series

Gill Ereaut, Mike Imms and Martin Callingham

This series of books explains the theory and practice of qualitative market research, or commercial qualitative research. There is no single agreed definition of qualitative market research but we can paraphrase some key definitions and describe it thus:

> A form of market research that seeks to explore and understand people's attitudes, motivations and behaviours – the 'why' and 'how' behind the 'what' – using methods that seek to reach understanding through dialogue and evocation (rather than measurement). Qualitative research generally attempts to make sense of and interpret phenomena in terms of the meanings people bring to them.

In UK practice, which forms the focus of this series, the most common form of qualitative market research employs the group discussion (or 'focus group') and depth interview as its major field methods, although many other methods can be and are increasingly used, such as observational approaches.

Common to all methods is the aim of getting beyond public, conscious factors – those things that people can and will say in response to simple questions. Qualitative market research provides effective ways of exploring such issues as private thoughts and feelings, pre-conscious factors (such as intuitive associations, the taken-for-granted, habitual and culturally derived attitudes and behaviours), and the important issue of emotions. Also used within qualitative market research are techniques that enable researchers to overcome the limitations of the verbal.

The main objectives of qualitative market research usually involve one or more of the following:

- **Diagnosis** – providing depth of understanding of a current situation, of why things are the way they are.
- **Prognosis** – providing guidance on likely responses to options, plans or proposals.

- **Creativity** – using respondents in qualitative market research as a source of ideas, innovation and inspiration.

What users of qualitative market research have in common is a need for *understanding and sense-making*.

- It aims to reveal deep and specific understanding of activities, choices and attitudes relevant to client concerns across a range of stakeholders. These stakeholders are not simply consumers and customers, users of the goods and services of commercial organisations – increasingly qualitative market research is used by a wide range of not-for-profit organisations.
- The insights generated include an understanding of the interrelationships of issues, as well as the detail of individual issues.
- Qualitative market research offers a conceptual and not just descriptive view of these issues.
- It may also serve to codify tacit and informal knowledge of the external world and make it accessible to organisations.

It is hard to pinpoint the exact date and place of birth of commercial qualitative research but essentially it is a phenomenon of the post-Second World War era and arose in response to changing information needs of organisations. Initially it was marketers who began to recognise that meeting consumer wants and needs required a level of understanding of people's motivations, usage and attitudes that went beyond measurement of the 'simple, hard facts' accessible to survey methods.

The qualitative market research profession has undoubtedly 'come of age' – with an established and respected role within the decision-making procedures of a wide and diverse variety of commercial, not-for-profit and public sector organisations across the globe. It is hard to find any *commercial* organisation that does *not* now use qualitative market research, but within the past decade or so the range of organisations using commercial qualitative market research to aid organisational decision-making has broadened considerably. Qualitative market research has become a valuable tool for anyone who needs to take account of any 'stakeholder' groups – not just consumers and customers but also staff, users of public services, supporters, voters, inmates and so on.

The evolution of the qualitative market research profession has several distinctive characteristics.

- It has apparently evolved in parallel with, but completely separately from, the academic qualitative research community which exists today across many disciplines in the social sciences and humanities.
- Relatively few textbooks have been written about qualitative market research and many external commentators have noted that the

profession has a sparse literature, and limited discussion of issues that
concern academic researchers, such as epistemology.

- The early qualitative market researchers drew on a body of theory
  that came principally from psychology, but over the decades this has
  broadened to include other social sciences disciplines and methods
  (anthropology, sociology, cultural analysis, semiotics etc.), as well as continuing to develop methodology from emergent trends in psychology.
- Theory has tended to be incorporated and used in qualitative market
  research in a 'serendipitous' way. Few qualitative market researchers
  have been interested in theory for its own sake, but only for its utility
  value, applicability and usefulness in meeting clients' needs for relevant information and insights. A key characteristic of commercial
  qualitative market research is its eclecticism and important benefits
  arise from this *absence* of theoretical or methodological purism.

Why has this series been created? First, the industry has an essentially
'oral' tradition and a major aim of this series has been to record this tradition in written form. Simply setting down what is common practice, along
with beliefs about why things are done like this, has not been done before
in such a comprehensive way. Like all oral traditions, that of the qualitative research industry sometimes lacks consistency and its 'narrators' do
not always agree on its origins. We make no apology for the fact that the
reader will find evidence of this in slightly differing accounts and differing attributions of key principles. One of the benefits of creating this series
is that such differences become manifest and can be debated and perhaps
reconciled by future writers on commercial qualitative market research.

Secondly, as the industry has grown in size and matured, and as its
body of (largely tacit) knowledge has grown and broadened, the link
between the theories originally informing it and day-to-day practice has
tended to weaken. The limited interest in questions of methodology and
theory for their own sake warrants comment – and there are probably two
main reasons for this.

- First, the nature of clients' demand for commercial qualitative market
  research means that its value rests solely on the value of the *findings
  themselves* – rather than the detailed means of reaching those findings.
- Secondly, client organisations have, for the same reason, consistently
  shown little interest in theory – it has restricted commercial value in
  commercial qualitative market research.

This is in contrast to much academic qualitative research, where the
contributions of a study to methodological and theoretical knowledge
may be regarded as at least as valuable as the substantive findings themselves, and certainly need to be reported. There is now more interest
within qualitative market research in understanding the roots of everyday practice in order to enhance training and professional development.

Thus a second key aim of this series is to attempt to re-connect practice to theory.

Commercial qualitative market research has until very recently focused almost, though not entirely, on interview-based methods – 'groups and depths'. This is quite different from much academic qualitative research, which draws on a far broader range of methods. Here again, the reasons have to do with the nature of the demand for commercial qualitative market research. In short, the commercial qualitative market research industry has very effectively 'systematised' interview-based qualitative procedures. In consequence there is a large and established market *and* a commercially viable established 'going rate' for interview-based commercial qualitative research that simply does not exist, at least at present, for other methods.

Within the limitations of interviewing methods, commercial qualitative market research has been incredibly creative. This creativity ranges from the application of sophisticated projective and enabling techniques and extensive use of stimulus material, to differing moderating styles, interview lengths, structures and procedures to extend the boundaries of what can be explored and captured within 'groups and depths'.

The qualitative market research business has developed specialisms, involving specific theories, methods and ideas of best practice:

- relating to particular types of respondents – children, business-to-business, staff etc.
- relating to particular types of topic – social policy, advertising development, new product development, packaging design, design and layout of stores, branch offices and websites etc.
- relating to specific business sectors – for example the pharmaceutical industry makes extensive use of qualitative market research, but tends to use quite tailored interview procedures and sampling methods, and specialist moderators.

Representing the full range of practice across all these fields is beyond the scope of this series, which aims to cover the primary research processes within mainstream practice, and two of the major applications of qualitative market research – the development of brands and the development of advertising. To the extent that many general principles, and certain aspects of practice, are shared across many varieties of qualitative market research, it will nevertheless be of relevance to many of these specialists.

The series has been written for the benefit of four main types of reader.

- First, **practitioners** (including those new to the profession) constitute a major audience for the series. By spelling out the key theories and principles that underpin good practice we hope practitioners can use this knowledge to train future generations of qualitative researchers – and also to make more informed choices of methodology and practice. By tracing back relevant theory and linking it to current practice, we aim to raise the conscious competence of current and future practitioners.

- Secondly we hope users of qualitative market research will find the series interesting and that it will enable them to make more informed assessments about the kind of contribution qualitative market research can make to organisational decision-making. It should also help them assess the quality of qualitative market research provided by their agencies and to recognise *good* qualitative market research.
- Thirdly, **students** of business and related disciplines may find it a helpful aid to understanding the role and value of qualitative market research in decision-making and how it works in real life practice.
- Finally, **academic qualitative researchers** may find the insight into commercial qualitative market research informative, given that so little is published about it. Commercial confidentiality means that the findings of few commercial qualitative market research projects will ever be made available, but this series at least exposes the principles and practice of qualitative market research in general terms.

In a more general sense, we hope that by being more explicit about what we do and why we do it, we can encourage constructive criticism. Specifically we hope to stimulate debate and to challenge others to identify better and different methods and practices.

All the books in this series have been written by respected qualitative market research practitioners, and as editors we are pleased that an unexpected benefit has arisen. The act of creating this series often involved analysing and setting down current practice for the first time. In so doing, a level of understanding of our business has emerged which was not evident to any of us before undertaking this comprehensive task. This emergent theory is described within several of the books in the series.

THE SCOPE OF THIS SERIES

The series comprises seven books, covering three broad categories. All the books are written primarily from a UK perspective, but where appropriate, authors have drawn comparisons with other markets, especially the USA.

- Book 1 provides an **introduction to qualitative market research** which contextualises the rest of the series. It also explores why it is that organisations might need qualitative market research and how it fits with their information needs and decision-making processes. This book, in addition, explores important issues not specifically addressed in other volumes, including the detail of project design, and the ethics and professional codes which underpin practice.
- Four other volumes describe the theory and methods of the key **processes** of commercial qualitative market research: interview-based fieldwork (Book 2); other forms of data collection (Book 3); analysis

and interpretation of findings (Book 4); and the development and 'delivery' of recommendations to clients (Book 7).
- Two further volumes – Books 5 and 6 – describe the theory and methods of two of the most significant **applications** of commercial qualitative market research – brand and advertising development.

Before going on to outline the scope and role of this particular book in the series, we would like to acknowledge the many people who helped in different ways to make this series a reality. We would particularly like to thank David Silverman for introducing us to Sage and for encouragement at the early stages; and the team at Sage, especially Michael Carmichael and Vanessa Harwood, for their support.

About this Book

Book 1 of this series explains how the core of QMR practice lies in interviewing methods and examines the continuing dominance of 'groups and depths' within qualitative market research practice. However, it is clear that not only have commercial researchers always been inventive *within* this interviewing format (a theme explored by Joanna Chrzanowska in Book 2), but in the past few years they have been more inventive and experimental *outside* it as well.

There has of course been spontaneous inventiveness of method within the industry as researchers search for better ways to address increasingly complex client problems. In addition, the specific demands of client organisations have evolved and whole new categories of clients have appeared. Together, these influences have been manifest in a wide range of approaches, techniques and methods.

We therefore needed a book within this series that would explore these departures, explain their significance and set them in context of the qualitative market research business as a whole. This book thus looks at a wide variety of alternatives to standard 'groups and depths' and explores for each one how and why it has appeared within the domain of qualitative market research. It also looks at some of the practical and ethical issues that arise as a consequence.

It is true that some of these approaches, such as ethnography or semiotic analysis, are not 'new', but have been around in academia for many years. Others, like business use of the Internet, are new, but are not unique to qualitative market research. However, they all represent departures in practice from what had become standard approaches for qualitative market research.

One role of the incorporation of a wider range of methods has been to expand on the ways in which qualitative research traditionally attempts to directly understand the lives of respondents. So observation, especially as part of an interview-based project, has been an extremely important addition to methods in recent years.

Some developments, however, employ radically different sources of data and insight. So, for example, cultural analysis and semiotic analysis move away from direct analysis of people and their lives altogether, drawing on quite different kinds of data.

There are also methodological developments which reflect the evolving demands of client organisations, presenting researchers with opportunities to expand and develop their repertoire of methods. These would include the demand for help with creativity, innovation and predicting the future, which is a major concern of many marketing organisations. As internal cultures have changed, too, there has been demand in some areas for direct contact between respondent and client – a contact that researchers have been asked to mediate and facilitate. Finally, organisational and cultural changes within various non-profit or public sector fields have resulted in a demand for qualitative research in social and policy arenas, some of which requires a rather different approach to that traditionally taken by qualitative market research.

There was clearly some danger that this book, with its 'everything that isn't standard interviewing' brief, might emerge as a ragbag of disconnected trends and ideas. This is a danger that Philly Desai has very obviously, and skilfully, avoided. The book takes a number of trends and directions and clearly outlines their significance, thinking and practice. Some of these trends will be familiar to practising researchers, some less so, but they have not been gathered together like this before.

The book does also, though, take a broader conceptual view of how we might see these developments as connected and draws some general themes and conclusions about the direction being taken by qualitative market research and the opportunities and challenges it now faces.

Introduction: The Interview in Social and Market Research

This chapter outlines the history of interviewing within social science and market research, and the classic characteristics of qualitative market research interviews and group discussions. It reviews some of the methodological criticisms which have been levelled at interviewing as a method *per se*, and suggests that these have become more pressing because of changes in the marketing context over the Past ten to fifteen years. Finally, it indicates the methods that market researchers have drawn upon to address these criticisms, and outlines the structure of the book.

The interview has long been central to social and marketing research, both qualitative and quantitative. The first attempts to gather social statistics in the mid-nineteenth century were based on interviews, as were the first sample surveys conducted in the 1920s (Tonkiss 1998). In the inter-war years, there was a growth in quantitative research in the UK, conducted by the government and also market research companies, with increasing attention paid to sampling methods, questionnaire design and standardisation of interviewing techniques. However, the limitations of large-scale quantitative surveys became increasingly apparent through the 1950s and 1960s, and qualitative methods grew in popularity as a way to overcome these limitations.

The 'interpretivist reaction against quantitative methodology' (Seale 1998: 204) drew upon different theoretical traditions in the social and market research worlds, although both were addressing similar problems. In both fields, quantitative research was criticised as providing a superficial picture of people's feelings and attitudes, with responses being strongly subjected to social pressure, and often bearing little relationship to what people really felt and did. In the world of social science, the arguments centred around the conflict between a positivist view of reality – the social world is real, and social research can describe and measure it – and an interpretivist paradigm – the social world is constructed by social actors, and social research can explore those constructions but should not see them as objectively 'real'. Thus, in social science, qualitative interviewing often adopts a social constructionist perspective, and has its theoretical basis in phenomenology and ethnomethodology (Seale 1998). These are both theoretical perspectives which explore how the social world is constructed by people within it rather than treating social relations as natural or 'given'.

Commercial market researchers, in contrast, drew upon theories and practices derived from psychology and psychotherapy (Imms 2000; Schlackman 1989). Psychotherapy was concerned with helping people arrive at an understanding of their true motivations, via discourse with a therapist, in order to help them change their behaviour. The assumption was that although such motivations might not be apparent to the client, the client could become aware of them and explain them verbally. The appeal of this for marketers – to understand why people really bought their products, and what they really felt about their clients' advertising – is clear. Mike Imms (2000) has outlined the impact of humanistic psychology on qualitative market research interviewing, in particular the idea of 'non-directive interviewing' developed by Carl Rogers. The three key features of non-directive interviewing were:

- **Transparency:** the therapist and client need to be honest, truthful and authentic.
- **Unconditional positive regard:** the therapist needs to accept the client's perspective in a non-judgemental way, avoid revealing their own opinions or trying to provide answers to the client's questions.
- **Empathetic understanding via attentive listening:** creating an environment in which the client feels safe to express their feelings, actively listening and attending to the emotional responses as well as the rational. (From Imms 2000)

These aspects of the relationship between interviewer and interviewee have had a lasting influence on qualitative market research. Although in practice there are many different styles of interviewing and conducting group discussions, the psychotherapeutic model is important as an archetype of interviewing, and as the norm from which other approaches are viewed. The key characteristics of this norm in qualitative research interviewing are:

1 **The researcher adopts a passive role:** he or she does not offer opinions, answer questions, provide information about themselves, and does not judge or challenge the respondent. The researcher is there to absorb what is said, and ask open, non-directive questions.

2 **The respondent is largely kept in the dark:** the researcher does not tell the respondent what the objectives of the research are, or provide information about the topic under discussion. The assumption is that whatever the researcher needs to know is contained within the

respondent, and that for the researcher to offer information to the respondent might bias their responses.

3   **The data is primarily verbal:** the interaction is essentially discursive, based on the question and answer format. The respondent is rarely asked to do something, go somewhere, or carry out some tasks – the assumption is that people call *tell* you what you need to know.

It is from these features that many of the strengths of qualitative research derive. It can represent reality from the perspective of the respondent, without interfering with or biasing that perspective, in their own words and using their own concepts. However, these are the very features which have laid interviewing and group discussions open to criticism. The remainder of this chapter discusses the limitations of conventional group discussions and interviews, and is divided into two sections. The first is concerned with methodology and the status of interview data. The second looks at changes in the marketing world which have called into question traditional interviewing practices.

THE STATUS OF INTERVIEW DATA

There are longstanding concerns about the nature and status of interview data, which have been much debated within social science and, to a lesser degree, commercial market research. Clive Seale (1998) has outlined the issues eloquently, suggesting that interview data can be seen in at least two ways:

- as a **resource** for analysis, to find out about the interviewee, their feelings, attitudes and behaviour outside the interview context; and
- as a **topic** of analysis, to reveal how people construct images of them-selves, their motivations, and their identity through social interactions such as interviews.

As Seale points out, a key criticism levelled against interview data was that 'what people said in interviews was not necessarily what they did in practice' (Seale 1998: 204). This does not mean that people deliberately lie in order to mislead the researcher – although this may happen – but rather that there are sound sociological reasons why there might be a gap between claimed behaviour and actual behaviour. These reasons fall into three categories.

Interview as Narrative

The idea of narrative analysis of interview data is common in academic social science, although much less so in commercial market research.

The key principle is that the interview is viewed as a story which a person tells about themselves, rather than as a transparent account of events, attitudes or feelings. This story is constructed retrospectively, as we build up a picture of who we are and what is important in our personal history by selectively choosing and omitting aspects of our past. These stories are sometimes called 'moral tales' (Silverman 1993: 108), as they usually present the interviewee as a moral and competent individual. What they do not provide is an objective account of social facts external to the interview context. On first sight, it might be thought that such a view of interview data would be of limited value to a commercial researcher, but that is not necessarily the case. If we were interviewing young men on what brands of beer they drink and why, we could see the interview as providing an insight into culturally acceptable reasons for brand preference, and forms of behaviour which were seen as high and low status among this group. It could provide insight into the language the young men use to describe and construct themselves, what events and situations they use to define their consumption patterns. However, we could not view the interview as unproblematically telling us what beers the young men drink, or why. To do that, we would need to observe their actual behaviour rather than ask them about it.

Social Pressures and Self-Image

Another common criticism of interview data is that respondents are subject to social pressures to answer in a certain way. Indeed, these pressures might be amplified in group discussions, where the respondent has to reveal themselves to the researcher and a number of other strangers as well. For example, when one compares how frequently people claim to brush their teeth or have a bath with the actual sales figures for toothpaste and soap, it is clear that interviewees may over-claim when describing socially desirable behaviour. The interview, in this context, does not provide a straightforward account of what people do, but rather gives people an opportunity to present themselves as they would like to be seen by others.

Self-Awareness and Memory

Implicit within the interview format – and the psychotherapeutic theory it rests on – is the assumption that people are, or can become, aware of their actions and motivations. However, it is by no means certain that people are consciously aware of what they are doing or why they are doing it. Recent thinking in both social anthropology (Bloch 1991; Bourdieu 1980) and neuroscience (Fletcher and Morgan 2000; Franzen and Bouwman 2001; Gordon 2001) has pointed out that much of the time people behave according to habit rather than conscious intent or motivation (indeed, this point was made by Alan Hedges in 1974 in his seminal work *Testing to Destruction*). Although we know how to make our way through a crowded bar, how to catch a barman's eye in a busy pub, or how to start our cars in the morning, these activities are not processed in the brain at a conscious level which allows us to recall them easily. Our understanding of how we do these things is implicit and we are rarely called upon to verbalise this understanding. If we are therefore asked about these things in interviews away from the context of the behaviour, we may find it hard to describe exactly how we carry out these habitual actions, or why we do them in the way we do. If we want to recall and discuss these actions, we need to enact them once again to activate the parts of the brain in which they are processed.

In addition to the issue of habitual action, there are also actions that have such a low level of involvement that the idea of motivation may be inappropriate to describe them – shoppers might purchase a particular brand of tea because it was easier to reach than another, or because there was a promotion – but asking people why they did this is unlikely to elicit this information. People are unlikely to remember such trivial decisions or low-level marketing cues, although they may retrospectively rationalise their behaviour in order to present themselves as sensible, normal shoppers. Robert Heath (2000) has termed this 'low involvement processing', and suggests that much advertising and branding works at this level of consciousness – without a high level of active involvement on the part of the consumer. Heath emphasises that these are not unconscious or subconscious processes, rather they are just not seen as very important by the conscious mind, and so are quickly forgotten. To research such processes, one needs to be very close to the point of consumption, as retrospectively these influences may never be recalled.

Ethical Concerns

Finally, the interview process has been criticised as exploitative and unethical. These criticisms centre around how the respondent is treated in the interview process and the relationship between the researcher and respondent. In academia, feminists such as Anne Oakely (1981) and Jane Finch (1984) have pointed out that there is often an unequal power relationship between interviewer and interviewee: the interviewer is in control of the agenda, asks the respondent to reveal themselves but does not reciprocate, demands information but does not provide it, wants the respondent to be open and honest but rarely does the same. Feminist researchers have suggested not only that such practices are unethical, but that they also result in bad research, as such an unequal relationship is unlikely to produce a truly open and trusting conversation. Commercial researchers too have been concerned about exploitation and deception of respondents, and many (Gordon 1999b; Humphries 2001) now argue that respondents should be seen as active partners in the research process, rather than passive subjects.

These methodological concerns are not new: indeed, they have been expressed since at least the 1960s. However, they appear to have become more pressing over the past decade or so as a result of changes in the world of marketing which have thrown these limitations into relief. Thus, not only are there methodological concerns expressed by research practitioners, there are also commercial concerns expressed by research buyers about the limitations of interview-based qualitative methods, especially approaches based on the passive, psychotherapeutic model. Whilst few research buyers or practitioners believe that the days of group discussions and individual interviews are numbered, there appears to be an increasing dissatisfaction with market research among buyers (Spackman et al. 2000). Research clients criticise research agencies as being too slow, obsessed with technique and quality control issues, delivering too much data and not enough insight, and not able to translate their findings into recommendations for action. Whilst there is some evidence that these criticisms are more likely to be levelled at quantitative research (White et al. 1997), qualitative research is not entirely free of these tendencies. In some cases, this has led clients to look elsewhere for real insight, in particular to management consultants, branding agencies or new product development (NPD) agencies. And indeed, many qualitative research agencies are also aiming to provide these more 'upstream' services, such as brand strategy and new product development. We shall now go on to discuss the changes in the marketing context which may have contributed to the relative downgrading of research, and look at the specific implications of these changes for practising researchers.

MARKETING IN A POSTMODERN AGE

Consumer marketing and research have not escaped from the all-pervasive influence of postmodernism, in terms of social theory, identity and key marketing concepts. Social theorists such as Harvey (1989), Bauman (1991) and Jameson (1991) have commented on a range of shifts in how society works, with the key features of the postmodern condition being:

- The decline of single sources of moral and intellectual authority.
- The ever-faster pace of change (technological and social).
- The destablisation of identity, e.g. more fluid concepts of social class, women adopting traditionally male roles.
- The fragmentation of society and community into smaller social units.
- The constant need for innovation and newness, sometimes referred to as 'hyperproduction' (Jameson, 1991).

This context of rapid social change, declining trust in authority and increasing fluidity in identity has created challenges for research. Both qualitative and quantitative research have traditionally relied on relatively fixed categories of identity which are assumed to remain stable over time, and to tell us something about the individuals to whom they are applied (for example, we think we know something about a consumer if we are told she is a female semi-skilled manual worker aged 30 with two children). However, a postmodern perspective would suggest that we need to be very careful about the assumptions we make based on these social categories.

Several authors have outlined the importance of these changes to marketing and to research specifically (Earls 2001; Gordon 1999b; Valentine and Gordon 2000; Smith and Dexter 2001). There appear to four key shifts in the context of marketing which relate to the postmodern condition:

- The speed of change and the impact of technology.
- The constant need to innovate.
- The increase in marketing literacy among consumers.
- The fluidity of categories of identity.

There are also two other trends which are not directly related to postmodernism, but which have more to do with developments in retail and branding:

- The rise of retailer power and category management.
- The emphasis on 'experiential' branding.

We shall now discuss each of these in turn.

The Speed of Change

Both Gordon (1999b) and Smith and Dexter (2001) place great emphasis on the increase in the pace of change within marketing. A huge amount of information is almost instantly accessible to the marketer, with recent developments such as Computer Assisted Interviewing and Internet surveys meaning that topline results of research are available on a daily basis. The problem, it is argued, is not getting access to information, but prioritising it and knowing what to do with it. Similarly, changes in consumer taste are thought to take place very quickly – what is 'in' today may be 'out' in three months' time – particularly in markets such as fashion, toys, technology or music. This means that marketers feel the need to be directly in touch with consumers, in order to judge what new products to launch and what style and tone of voice to adopt. The long timescales of some research projects may simply not be feasible, and many clients are demanding that research agencies find ways to give them a more direct and immediate experience of the consumer.

Innovation

The rapid pace of change has brought with it a constant desire to innovate. Indeed, it seems to be now accepted wisdom among many commercial marketers that innovation lies at the heart of a successful company (Gordon 1999b; Hirshberg 1998). If most consumer goods now function perfectly adequately, choices between brands may be made on the basis of small differences that have a big impact on the bottom line. Thus, companies appear to be forever looking for something new or different to distinguish their product, leading to situations where, as Mark Earls (2001) points out, the average UK consumer is faced with 50 different toothbrushes to choose from in the supermarket. Whilst research agencies are frequently called upon to help in the process of innovation, conventional qualitative methods have repeatedly been accused of stifling rather than facilitating creative thought and new ideas (Earls 2001; Gordon 1999b; Holder and Young 1997; Woods 1999).

The Marketing-Literate Consumer

The relationship between the consumer and the brand is also thought to have undergone considerable change. Historically, the role of branding has been to provide consumers with reassurance – a mark of quality and legitimacy to bridge the gap that was created between the consumer and the manufacturer by the industrial production process (De Chernatony and McDonald 1998). This was essentially a paternalistic relationship, where the consumer trusted the brand owner. However, current consumers, it is argued, are less likely to 'take things on trust' and they are more knowing and cynical about marketing and advertising. This, it has been argued (Pillot De Chenecey 2000), means that brands need to gain consumers' respect and acquire legitimacy within their lives, and that if people feel brands are 'trying to trick them with advertising' they will quickly reject the message. These marketing-literate consumers need to be treated as knowledgeable partners in the research process, if they are not to be alienated by outdated approaches that assume a naïve consumer.

The Fluidity of Identity

The increasing fluidity of social identity means that concepts such as 'target audience' or 'consumer segmentation' need careful rethinking. Within social theory (e.g. Hall 1992) and marketing theory (Valentine and Gordon 2000), there has been a shift away from thinking of identity as a fixed, stable social fact, towards seeing it as a process that is constantly recreated by individual actors in particular social contexts. Thus, any one individual may have a range of identities which they deploy at different times, in different contexts – father, lover, son, business person, one of the lads. Global communications have opened up a much wider range of identity options – a middle-class white teenager in an English suburb may speak the language of urban black youths in New York – and there is also an increasing fluidity with which these identities are chosen. In the context of consumption, as Gordon and Valentine have argued, this means that individuals cannot be seen as 'brand loyal'; rather, they may use different brands within a category to fulfil different aspects of their identity. The implication for consumer segmentation is a shift from dividing individuals into groups who can be targeted, towards dividing the different identities which any one individual might adopt within a category – what the Henley Centre call 'modal segmentation', or 'need.states' according to The Research Business. To research these forms of identity requires more work at the point of consumption, including observational and ethnographic methods, probably spending more time with a smaller number of consumers.

There are two other key shifts in the marketing context which are relevant, but less directly linked to issues of postmodernity:

The Growth of Retailer Power

The increasing power of the large retailers, and the growth of the discipline of category management, are two related issues which have had a great impact on manufacturers (Fletcher and Morgan, 2000; Johnson and Pinnington, 1998). Category management refers to the way in which retailers manage the range of brands within a product field – frozen desserts, coffee, biscuits – in order to maximise consumer choice and avoid duplication. As Fletcher and Morgan suggest, the manufacturer has had to pay more attention to the shopping experience, and to the whole category within which their brand exists – a focus on consumption and on individual brands is no longer sufficient.

Category management has also led to an increased need to conduct research in store, and to view any one brand or product in a broader context. Retailers and manufacturers are increasingly working in partnership to maximise consumption within entire categories. It therefore becomes more important to understand the relationships between different brands, rather than to focus on brands in isolation.

The Enlargement of the 'Brand Experience'

Finally, there is the recent growth in the idea of 'brand experiences'. This refers to the desire of brand owners to control the entire experience the consumer has when interacting with their brand, and by extension to associate brands with particular experiences (Jones 2000). Brand owners such as Nike, Disney, Starbucks and The Gap, for example, are concentrating at least as much of their efforts on the retail experience – the point of sale, the display of the products, the architecture and décor of the store, the attitude and appearance of their staff – as on the actual product. Indeed, as Naomi

Klein (2000) has demonstrated, many international brands now see their business primarily as creating the brand image, whilst the creation of the product is entirely outsourced. As with the increase in retailer power referred to above, this trend means that marketers need increasingly to understand how the consumer experiences the brand in context. Whereas in the past a sports clothing manufacturer might have wanted to be seen as the most stylish, prestigious, or whatever, now they are more likely to want to own the experience of 'participating in sport', or of 'aspiration'. From a research point of view this clearly requires a much wider perspective, to see how the brand functions in the context of a whole lifestyle as well as in its product or category context.

CONCLUSIONS

There have long been debates about the limitations of interview data within the social sciences, and these methodological concerns have recently been heightened by the impact of postmodernism on patterns of consumption. These changes in the marketing context have called into question the archetypal model of qualitative research interviewing, derived from humanistic psychotherapy. This model was originally developed to gain an understanding of attitudes, feelings and motivations, but it is now used to explore a much wider range of issues. Many researchers have developed different ways of working with groups and individuals to address these concerns, and have also drawn on alternative methods which may be better adapted to answer the new questions being asked of researchers. In some cases, qualitative market researchers have drawn upon ideas from other disciplines to adapt the ways in which they work with groups, whilst in others these methods may be used instead of conducting group discussions or individual interviews. The remainder of this book discusses these approaches. In the final chapter we shall address the implications of these developments for the future of qualitative market research.

KEY POINTS

- The interview is central to social and market research, although there are longstanding questions about the nature of interview data.
- Potential problems include:
  - The idea that interviews might be best seen as 'moral tales', narratives that provide the interviewee with the opportunity to construct a certain self-image.

- o Problems with remembering and describing actions which are processed in the brain in ways that are hard to recall.
- o Ethical concerns about the relationship between researcher and respondent, which can be seen as exploitative and deceitful.

- There have also been changes in the marketing context which have thrown into relief the limitations of conventional approaches to interviewing. These include:

- o The speed of change in some markets means that companies increasingly value direct, immediate contact with their consumers.
- o Consumers are more marketing-literate and cynical about advertising and branding.
- o Conventional ideas about social identity are breaking down and consumer identities are more fluid.
- o The increasing focus on lifestyle and the 'brand experience' means that marketers need to understand how their brands fit into consumers' lives as a whole.

- These changes have meant that more flexible approaches to interviews and group discussions have been developed, as well as alternative methods which supplement conventional interview-based research.

Observation and Ethnography

This chapter discusses the uses of observational and ethnographic methods in commercial marketing research. It starts by outlining the strengths of observational methods compared with interviews and group discussions, and the history of their use in academic and commercial research. It then goes on to explore the areas in which observation and ethnography can be most useful: targeting hard-to-reach groups, exploring topics where there is a strong social pressure to conform, exploring the retail environment, lifestyle issues, habitual or low involvement actions, and product usage. Some of the key areas of debate within current thinking on observational research are outlined and the chapter concludes by discussing the practical implications of this for commercial researchers.

OBSERVATION, ETHNOGRAPHY AND MARKET RESEARCH

Observational and ethnographic research methods are increasingly used in commercial market research, although they have long been common within anthropology and sociology. In commercial research, they are frequently used as an addition to conventional qualitative methods, although some researchers do use them as stand alone methodologies (for example, Siamack Salari at EverydayLives in the UK, and Hy Mariampolski at Qualidata in New York). The appeal of observational research for marketers and commercial researchers it that it is seen to overcome the key issue that has vexed interview data for years: the problem that what people say, and what they actually do, may be two different things. By observing actual behaviour in its social context, many of the problems discussed in the previous chapter can be partly overcome. Indeed, Mariampolski has gone so far as to suggest that 'Ethnography is the truth serum of research' (1999), and has accounted for its popularity among marketers by pointing out that it is 'the closest that the market researcher can get to the consumer' (1997). Siamack Salari and Kirsty Fuller have also suggested that the backlash against 'focus groups' has made marketers keen to get out of the viewing facility and into the real world, and to talk to 'real people' rather than professional respondents. Also, observational data can make a greater impact than conventional research debriefs – seeing is believing, after all – and many companies now run 'Consumer Connection' programmes for their staff to engage in direct contact with their consumers.

This chapter discusses the uses of observational and ethnographic methods in qualitative market research, and suggests how these approaches can address some of the issues raised in Chapter 1. First, the history of observational methods in social and commercial research is outlined and the range of approaches available described. Then the areas in which observational methods have proved most useful to commercial marketers are discussed and the important question of the extent to which observational research may change the behaviour being observed is addressed. The chapter concludes by discussing the practical challenges posed to commercial researchers who wish to conduct observational research, and suggests how these methods can be combined with more conventional groups and interviews.

Historical Perspective

As pointed out above, ethnographic and observational methods are not new. Indeed, there is a long history of people from one cultural background spending time with a different cultural group in order to understand their language, beliefs and values. Christian Gatard (2001) has traced the history of qualitative research back to the early Greeks Tacitus and Herodotus, although most conventional histories of ethnography begin with the nineteenth century and the records of missionaries and administrators from the West in the colonial period (Vidich and Stanford 2000). Here, information about local customs, languages, religions and beliefs was gathered by the colonists in order to set up administrative and financial systems in the newly acquired colonies, as well as out of an interest in so-called 'primitive peoples'. This early ethnography became more formalised within the discipline of anthropology, which grew substantially in the first half of the twentieth century. Many of the founding fathers of British social anthropology worked during this period (Malinowski 1922; Evans-Pritchard 1940), and the classic characteristics of ethnographic research – long-term immersion in a different culture, living with the people and learning their language – were established.

In addition to the ethnography of 'primitive' or 'exotic' peoples, ethnographic research was also used closer to home, in both the UK and the USA. In the UK, the social reformer Charles Booth carried out extensive fieldwork researching his series on *The Life and Labour of the People in London* (1905), whilst in the USA many studies of the urban environment of Chicago were carried out between 1920 and 1940 by the sociologist Robert Park and his colleagues (Park et al. 1925).

In the UK, Mass Observation was set up in the 1930s and conducted studies of British social life using ethnographic methods during the 1930s and 1940s (Deegan 2001; Pegram and Lee 2000). Mass Observation sent teams of trained observers into people's houses and recorded them living their day-to-day lives. According to Deegan, the organisation started as a radical sociological project but by the 1950s was working as a commercial research organisation. And in the 1970s, large manufacturing companies such as Unilever were observing people cooking and taking baths in their research laboratories (Pegram and Lee 2000).

Thus, observation is not new, although it is increasing in popularity. In part, this is due to the dissatisfactions with conventional qualitative methods outlined in the previous chapter, although it does also appear to fit into a broader cultural trend. Fly-on-the-wall documentaries, 'reality TV' shows such as *Big Brother* and *Survivor*, Consumer Connection programmes run by many companies – all show the level of interest in unmediated reality. Indeed, they seem to reflect a quest for authenticity, a desire to see the unvarnished 'truth' as opposed to the myriad of competing media representations whose veracity is hard to assess. Observational methods and data fit into this wider trend, and it is likely that they are therefore more easily understood and, perhaps, believed by marketers and researchers alike.

The Spectrum of Approaches

As the discussion above suggests, there is a wide range of approaches that can be termed observational or ethnographic research. With academic sociology and anthropology, the most common way of describing this range is as a spectrum with four main divisions, depending on the researcher's level of involvement with the subjects of the research (Walsh 1998).

1 **Complete observer:** the researcher observes but does not interact with the research subjects. Indeed, the subjects usually do not know they are being observed, for example via the use of a fixed camera in a supermarket aisle, or observing crowd behaviour at a football match. This ensures that the subjects are not affected by being observed, but offers little opportunity to understand their motivations, values and attitudes.
2 **Observer as participant:** the researcher observes behaviour and tries to avoid influencing the subjects, although they may occasionally ask questions to clarify confusions or gain practical information.
3 **Participant as observer:** the researcher tells the research subjects that he or she is a researcher and explains the research process. The emphasis is on interacting with people, developing relationships and gaining understanding through participating in their lives.
4 **Complete participant:** the researcher works covertly to gain access to a group and participate in their lives, without revealing their real

identity or research agenda. This method can be useful in researching highly secretive groups, such as cults, criminal groups or extreme political organisations (Renzetti and Lee 1993). It has also been used among powerful groups who might not allow researchers to work with them, for example studies of sexism among city traders, or racism in the police.

In practice, most ethnographic research is conducted in the middle of this spectrum. This is because the researcher wants to explore people's beliefs, attitudes and cultural values as well their behaviour, and this necessitates some degree of interaction between the researcher and the researched. Without this interaction, it is difficult to gather any but the most basic behavioural data, and the researcher also runs the risk of misinterpreting people's actions and motivations. Complete participation, on the other hand, creates ethical and practical problems which rule it out for many commercial studies, as discussed below.

Thus, ethnographic research is characterised by the following features:

- A focus on the cultural and social context of people's actions and beliefs – looking at people as whole individuals, rather than compartmentalised consumers.
- Seeing the world from the point of the view of the participants, and avoiding imposing the researchers' cultural frameworks.
- Allowing people to use their own language to describe their world.
- Looking at behaviour in the place and time at which it actually occurs – in the home, the office, the car, the supermarket.
- A long-term involvement with individuals or groups.
- The use of a range of data collection methods, including interviews, group discussions, informal conversations and observations of behaviour, and also the inclusion of cultural artefacts as part of the data – e.g. photographs, films, drawings.

Ethnography, then, is firmly rooted in the qualitative research tradition, and has its theoretical roots in a social constructionist view of culture. This means that it looks at how human societies give meaning to their actions within specific cultural frameworks, and at how these cultural frameworks interact with larger social structures such as economics, history, politics and geography.

THE USES OF OBSERVATIONAL AND ETHNOGRAPHIC METHODS

There are marketing areas in which observational methods have proved particularly helpful, and we look here, first, at the **target audiences** and **product fields** in which observational approaches may be advantageous. These include target audiences that are hard to reach via conventional qualitative methods (e.g. nightclubbers) and markets where there is a strong social pressure to conform or 'say the right thing' (e.g. healthy eating). In the second section we will outline a range of **marketing issues** which are particularly amenable to observation.

Target Audiences

Irrespective of the topic of the research, there are some target audiences for whom ethnographic or observational approaches may be particularly useful. These include people who are hard to access, who may not feel happy in a group discussion or interview, or who lead lifestyles which make it difficult to keep appointments. The most common groups who are thought to fall into this category are various youth segments, in particular so-called 'leading edge' consumers – young people who are at the forefront of trends in fashion, music and social identity. Whilst it may not be impossible to invite these young people to a conventional group discussion, more informal mechanisms may work better. Kirsty Fuller of Flamingo, an international research consultancy based in London, says that they initially started using ethnographic methods because they could not access the young people they needed via conventional recruitment methods. They wanted to talk to nightclub-goers, people who went to 'squat parties', ecological activists, and garage music fans, but conventional research methods proved unsuccessful. As Kirsty Fuller recalls:

> The start point was actually a recruitment issue which was for a particular client. They wanted us to recruit what they described as leading edge youth, and we just couldn't recruit those people through conventional methods. I think they weren't accessible because of the nature of the recruiters and methods of recruitment in the UK. Now, we have narrowed down the recruiters we use to one or two who do it tremendously well, and because they are leading edge themselves, they are respected amongst their contemporaries and they don't frame it as coming to a market research group, they just say 'are you going to come along for a chat' or something. And we also try to do them at home because that works better. It is less formal and less teacher-ish for them.

Fuller suggests that by working through more informal networks, presenting the exercise as an interesting chat rather than market research, and being willing to include groups of friends and do the fieldwork in the respondents' homes, they have been more successful working in these markets than via conventional research alone. Similarly, Gerry Hahlo of Informer Interactive, a youth-focused research consultancy based in London, argues that if researchers want to get the views of, say, young skateboarders, it is better to go and chat to them informally at their local skate park than to take them away to a viewing facility. The young people might be reluctant to attend a group, and they might be more articulate and forthcoming in an environment in which they feel comfortable.

Finally, research conducted by the author among heroin addicts in London in collaboration with Market Research Services, a London-based agency, used a flexible interviewing strategy. The researchers gained the trust of local drugs workers and gave them a rough specification of the range of individuals we wanted to include. We then hired a room in a local community centre, went there on a daily basis, and interviewed whoever the workers managed to recruit on that day. Clearly, the somewhat chaotic lifestyles of drug users would have made conventional recruitment and more formal approaches difficult to maintain. Also, they would probably have been suspicious of approaches from strangers, but the fact that our recruiters were local drugs workers meant they were trusted by the drug users.

Thus, a flexible approach to recruitment and to where and when fieldwork takes place can help researchers access people who might otherwise be excluded from research. The use of 'gatekeepers' from within the cultural group being explored is standard ethnographic research practice, and it clearly also has potential for commercial qualitative studies. This does not mean abandoning the group discussion or interview format, as in many cases a fully ethnographic approach would be incompatible with the research objectives. In the study of drug users mentioned above, it was initially suggested that the researchers should conduct the interviews in the corridors, basements and stairwells of local housing estates. However, this was not feasible because we needed to show respondents stimulus materials. Thus, the study was informed by an ethnographic perspective, but was not a fully ethnographic project.

Topics Subject to Social Pressures

Observational approaches can also be useful for topics where there are strong social, moral or legal pressures to act in a certain way. Where there is a clear 'right answer' people may be reluctant to admit their real behaviour if it does not conform to the socially acceptable norm. They may use the interview as a chance to construct a 'moral tale' rather than a straightforward account of their behaviour. Experienced qualitative researchers will try to minimise the effect of 'social desirability bias' and to take account of this in interpreting interview data, but observational approaches can provide a useful alternative source of data. Topics such as the following fall into this category.

- **Personal hygiene:** e.g. how frequently people wash, how much soap they purchase, how frequently they brush their teeth. These are areas in which people tend to over-claim, and surveys on these topics frequently overestimate the market for personal hygiene products.
- **Household cleaning:** over-claiming the frequency and thoroughness of cleaning the house is common, particularly as some women feel

morally judged on the cleanliness of their homes. Hy Mariampolski has referred to observational work conducted in the home (1997) where the researchers observed a woman cleaning the toilet bowl and the bathroom basin surface – where the toothbrushes were kept – with the same cloth. It is unlikely that she would have admitted to this in an interview.

- **Healthy eating practices:** most people now are well aware of healthy eating messages, and might not want to admit to regular snacking through the day. For example, Fiona Jack and Bas Homans (2000) interviewed health-conscious eaters about their diets, and then asked to look in their fridges to see what was really there. The research found that although respondents did indeed purchase the healthy foods they claimed, they also frequently had chocolate bars or other indulgences which were used as 'treats'.

- **Television viewing:** people frequently underestimate the amount of time they spend watching television. They may also underplay their viewing of soaps and game shows, and over-claim the time spent watching news and documentaries. Interestingly, in work conducted by British Telecom which measured the amount of time families spent in front of the television (BT Street 2, reported on *Channel 4 News*), the families themselves were suprised when they saw the results. This suggests that respondents were not attempting to deceive the researchers, but that their self-image was out of line with the reality of their behaviour.

In addition to topics where there is a social pressure to conform, there are also purchase processes where people have a tendency to rationalise retrospectively. For example, Fiona Jack and Bas Homans discuss a study of mobile phone choice among first-time purchasers. In interviews, people tended to overstate their own role in the purchase process, and to present a rationalised account of their purchasing behaviour. However, in-store observations found that first-time buyers typically chose the handset first, based on its look, feel and design, and then allowed the salesperson to take the lead on recommending which subscription to take out. And Paco Underhill (2000) points out that when purchasing CD players most people in a shop will open and close the lid as a way of judging how well made the product is, especially if there is no opportunity to listen to it. However, if interviewed afterwards about their reasons for purchasing a particular player, they would be more likely to talk about the technical specification than the satisfying clunk as it shuts!

Thus, there are certain target audiences or research topics where conventional interview-based methods can fail to access the right respondents, or provide a misleading account of people's real behaviour. However, by adopting a more flexible approach to recruitment, and by combining interviews with observational methods, researchers can provide richer and more accurate information about consumer behaviour.

We shall now move on to discuss marketing issues that lend themselves particularly to observational methods. We have divided these marketing issues into two broad categories:

- **Going wider:** looking at the physical and social contexts within which behaviour is embedded.
- **Going deeper:** looking in detail at the micro level of human behaviour, the routines and habitual actions to which we pay little or no attention.

Going Wider

Ethnographic and observational methods are particularly useful for exploring the social and cultural context of people's behaviour. Whilst interviews tend to focus on the product, brand or advertising, ethnographic work can explore the context within which products are used, brands understood and advertising consumed. For example, an interview or group discussion about beer might focus on brand imagery, user imagery, drinking occasions and taste preferences. An ethnographic approach would probably provide a fuller exploration of where people consume different brands, who they are with, what they talk about while drinking, what they are usually doing, what music is playing, and how beer drinking fits into the context of a night out. This might be most useful at the stage of developing an advertising or branding strategy, whilst more conventional group discussions would be better adapted, for example, to developing particular creative routes.

This section focuses on the exploration of spatial and social contexts under four headings: people and spaces, social contexts, lifestyles and shifting identities.

People and Spaces

The overall layout of a shop, bar, pub or even office is a subject highly amenable to observational research. One can analyse how different spaces are used, whether there are any 'dead spaces', how people flow through the space, the direction from which people look at products, and what sort of relationships are implied between staff and customers by the overall design. Paco Underhill (2000) provides many revealing examples of how observational research has guided the layout of stores and the positioning of products and displays. For example, he points out that in chemists' shops there are two directions of flow. Customers coming to get prescriptions tend to go straight to the pharmacy at the back of the shop, and then make other purchases on their way out. Customers without prescriptions shop the other way around – from the front of the shop to the back. Thus, some displays should face the front of the shop, and some should face the back. Similarly, in video rental shops people usually choose their film first, and then buy snacks afterwards or while queuing to take out their video. This means that films need to face the front of the shop, but snacks need to face the back as the customer is most interested in buying them when they are on their way out.

Layout can also influence the relationship established between staff and customers. For example, in a study of the design of Army Careers Information Offices conducted by the author, the desk of the Army Careers Officer was usually placed directly in front of the entrance. This meant that the potential recruit entering the office was immediately faced with a uniformed soldier, had little time to acclimatise to the military environment, and felt that they had to account for themselves as soon as they walked in. This was off-putting for young people who were less certain of their interest in an Army career. For example, when researchers accompanied one group of young women to the local recruitment office, some respondents approached the door, saw the soldier at the front desk, and quickly moved away without going in. The research suggested that the offices might benefit from a two-part spatial arrangement. First, there could be a reception area with leaflets, videos, CD ROMs and informal seating, where young people could gather information in their own time. Secondly, there could be a more formal area where the recruiters sat and where interviews and careers advice were offered, with the recruiters' desks set at an angle to the main entrance.

Pegram Walters used similar methods in helping a bank re-design its branches. First, a test branch was mocked up with the new design and layout. A sample of customers was invited in and was observed using the branch and interviewed afterwards. The observations quickly revealed that the area with comfortable chairs and leaflets on display was avoided by customers, although they did concentrate in the less attractive area around the cashpoint machines. Interviews quickly revealed that the 'nicer' part of the branch looked like the sort of place where people would try to sell you insurance, whilst the less well-appointed cashpoint area looked less threatening to customers. The designers were able to make amendments very quickly, and in the next phase of the research the new design did not suffer from these problems.

The Social Context

As well as exploring the spatial context of behaviour, observational research is also useful for exploring the social context – the interactions between different customers, and between customers and staff. In the case of retail outlets, people do not always shop alone, and many shopping trips will involve a degree of compromise between the different people involved – parents and children, men and women, or groups of friends. An understanding of this can help the retailer develop strategies that work with, rather than against, the social dynamics of shopping.

Paco Underhill (2000: 152) analysed the amount of time and money spent in clothes shops by teenagers in groups, and by teenagers accompanied by their parents. The groups of teenagers spent longer in the shops, and examined more products, but were half as likely to buy anything as the teenagers accompanied by their parents. This might have led the retailer to believe that they should discourage groups of teenagers from browsing without their parents. However, according to Underhill what was happening was that the teenagers visited with their friends to choose what they wanted, and once they had decided they made a quick visit with their wallet-bearing parents to buy it!

The relationship between parents and children shopping together has been subjected to much research. Clearly, retailers need to understand the influence of the children on parents' shopping habits, in order to assess to what extent they should target the parent with promotions and to what extent they should target the child. However, in group discussions parents tend to understate the influence of their children, suggesting that they would not acquiesce to children's demands for particular products. Observational research, however, suggests a more complex picture. Rust (1993a) conducted observational research in the USA on children and parents shopping together. Rust's methodology is not described in detail and does appear rather unreliable, but the project did offer interesting suggestions for marketing that could use the influence of the child without, hopefully, antagonising the parent:

- Put information in the shopping trolley for the child to look at, thus communicating marketing information and keeping the child occupied.
- Produce packaging and promotional material designed to be looked at in the shopping trolley by the child.
- Display products targeting children at the height of the child in the trolley.
- Select names for products which will be easy for children to say and read, and consider including educational material on packs, such as basic reading games.

All these marketing recommendations emerged from observations of children and parents shopping together, and they clearly emphasise the importance of the physical environment of shopping and the way in which packaging and promotions are used in the store.

Finally, of course, the relationship between staff and customers is an important part of the marketing mix. Underhill's work has shown that in many retail environments the most important predictor for purchase is whether the customer has any contact with a member of staff – if they do, they are much more likely to buy something. Thus, the nature of the inter-action between staff and customers can be very influential in terms of sales and also brand image. Pegram Walters in London have conducted various studies in the drinks market, and Scott Lee points out the impor-tance of observing how bar staff serve particular drinks. Do they always offer a certain brand if the choice is left to them? Do they offer a glass with one brand but not with another? Do they toss the bottle in the air with a flourish? All these can influence brand image and sales, but consumers are unlikely to remember or refer to such small-scale details if asked about a particular brand in interviews.

Lifestyle Issues

In addition to analysing the social and physical context of the retail environment, observational methods can also explore the ways in which brands and products fit into the lifestyles of their consumers. What roles do they play within particular experiences, occasions, or social events? How does the relationship between the consumer and brand come to life in real time, and what does this relationship mean to the consumer? All these questions are particularly important for youth and fashion brands which, reportedly, need to gain the 'respect' of the consumer and to be seen as a legitimate part of their social lives. Several new marketing tactics have developed to respond to these needs, with methods that engage directly with subcultural youth groups. For example, *Marketing Magazine* in May 2001 reports that Budweiser directly organise events called 'Bud House Parties', moving 'beyond sponsorship into events management and promotion', whilst Britvic Tango are 'challenging students to write their own ads for the brand'. And Naomi Klein (2000) gives many examples of other companies that pay young people to 'talk up' their brands among their peers. Youth and fashion markets move very fast, and a loss of credibility can cost brands dearly.

Thus, brand owners need to know exactly how their brands fit into the lifestyle of the people they are trying to attract. They need to know when and how brands are used, what feelings and contexts are associated with their brand, what sorts of social experiences are happening when their brand is being consumed, who else is likely to be there, what are they doing, and what they will be talking about. These questions are essential to create compelling and credible brands and advertising ideas, and they will be hard to answer without some use of observational or ethnographic methods. In the drinks market, for example, it is now quite common for researchers to go out with a group of young people who are consumers of the brand in question, spend the evening with them doing whatever they would normally do, and then convene a group discussion a week or so later to explore the issues in greater depth. This is because frequently what the brand owner is trying to do is to take ownership of a particular experience and associate it with their brand – therefore an experiential understanding of how the brand fits into consumer lifestyles is crucial. David Farrow of D'Arcy points out how using photography in combination with group discussions helped develop a positioning for an alcohol brand.

> We realised that this brand was seen as a beginning of the evening drink. What we looked at doing was actually getting people to photograph their best experience at the beginning of the evening, what the beginning of the evening meant to them and they'd bring that to the groups. So, that

photograph might have been someone in front of the mirror doing their hair and it might have been a picture of the boyfriend that they were going off to meet. It could have been anything, it could have been any event in the bar. Someone might say 'it is the beginning of the evening I really enjoy, because we all meet up at a particular café', or club, or bar or whatever. We use that to kind of find a tonality, and a commonality, because I think in drinks markets, one of the key things isn't so much what you say, it's how you say it, and what tone of voice you use, how up you are, how not up you are. We didn't spend an awful lot of time talking about the brand, it was more about their experiences.

Finally, certain retailers also need to explore how their retail outlets fit into the lifestyles of their customers, as the actual product sold is often a relatively small part of the 'brand experience'. Naomi Klein (2000) has outlined how brands such as Nike, The Gap, Borders and Starbucks do not see themselves solely as retailers of shoes, clothes, books or coffee. Rather, their marketing focuses on developing the brand as the marker of a particular lifestyle and set of values. They want to associate their brands with experiences or social events which are thought to be central to the value systems of their consumers. Starbucks, for example, has tried to develop the idea of the 'third space', the place between home and office where people meet their friends, socialise, relax, hang out and, presumably, drink expensive coffee. What is being consumed is not simply coffee – it is a whole brand experience which, ideally, should have some broader meaning and resonance within the value system of the consumer. Similarly, Borders presents itself as a place where intelligent sophisticated people go to relax, browse, attend readings and debates, and meet their friends, as well as buying books and CDs. Observational research in store, and with consumers in other contexts, can help evaluate the extent to which the retail environment is providing these experiences which are so important to the brand value.

Thus, adding an ethnographic component to conventional qualitative methods can help considerably when the researcher is trying to gain an understanding of a total lifestyle, again because ethnography looks at behaviour in its social and cultural context.

Shifting Consumer Identities

Thus far, we have looked at how observational methods can be focused on particular environments (shops, bars, banks, pubs) and social events (a night out, a trip to the shops) in order to evaluate how these spatial and social contexts affect behaviour. Finally, we can turn the question around and, instead of making the context the topic of investigation, focus on the changing consumer. As outlined in Chapter 1, consumer identities are increasingly fluid, brand loyalty is declining and people may use a range of different products or brands within a category. By focusing on individuals and following them over time in different contexts, ethnographic research can help identify the range of identity options within a particular category, and can help marketers ensure that their brands meet those different needs as fully as possible.

Let us put this in the marketing context more explicitly. A woman today might at different times be a wife, mother, lover, businesswoman, shopper and 'ladette' during the course of a single week – and it is unlikely that she would choose the same brand of hosiery or cosmetics for each occasion. Leith and Riley (1998) develop the useful concept of 'need.states' to describe these different identities, which they emphasise arise from a combination of contextual factors and internal emotional needs. Within particular categories – alcoholic drinks, underwear, snack foods, whatever – there is a finite range of 'need.states', and manufacturers and retailers need to understand these differing needs of the same consumer (this idea is discussed more fully in Chapter 5 on Cultural Analysis). This is particularly important, they suggest, in developing retail strategies for fast moving consumer goods (FMCGs). In the case of cosmetics, for example, they point out that on some occasions a woman (most of the examples given by Leith and Riley concern female shoppers) may want to get advice from a sales consultant if trying out a new product, whilst on other occasions she may simply want to put the usual mascara in her basket and go. Ideally the retail environment should provide for both these needs, rather than forcing the consumer to talk to the salesperson whether she wants to or not. Similarly, in the case of hosiery, a woman may have quite different needs if she is going for a business meeting, compared with an anniversary dinner, and this might suggest not only different products or brands, but also different retail environments and sales methods.

Ethnographic research can be useful for identifying these different needs because it views the consumer in different contexts and at different times. These features of ethnographic research can make it better adapted to revealing the range of behaviours which any one person may engage in within particular categories – a range that might be smoothed over in interviews or group discussions in the interests of presenting a reasonably consistent picture of oneself. Leith and Riley suggest that a range of methods, including group discussions, accompanied shopping and observing the actual activity being explored, are all useful in identifying 'need.states' and analysing the influence of context on people's actions. Paul Edwards of The Henley Centre has also suggested that, in future, researchers will need to spend more time with a smaller number of people, rather than the quantitative tradition of spending very little time with a large number of people (Observational Research Forum Seminar, London, September 2000). As he comments, the same person can be more different at two points in time, than two different people at the same point in time.

Going Deeper

Thus, observational and ethnographic methods are very useful for widening the focus of research, going beyond the brand or product to the social and physical context in which they are purchased and used. These contextual factors are often very important in explaining aspects of brand image or sales patterns, but they are hard to explore in conventional research methods where people are removed from the context of their behaviour.

However, observation can also provide rich insights when focused on the minutiae of human behaviour – a zoom lens rather than a wide-angle view. Here, observation can provide insights into habitual actions of which we may not be aware; it can reveal that the influence of sales promotions at the point of sale may not be consciously noticed; and it can show the ways in which products are used in the real world, rather than in the laboratory. This section discusses the use of observational methods to focus on the detail rather than the big picture.

Low Involvement Processing

Robert Heath (2000) has developed the idea of 'low involvement processing' as a means of explaining the influence of advertising and point of sale promotions. Heath argues that most marketing and advertising messages are seen as trivial and unimportant by the consumer, and that little conscious attention is paid to them. On the contrary, the brain deals with these messages quickly and with limited involvement. Heath does not suggest that these messages are processed subconsciously, but rather that they are accorded very little attention and, once dealt with, are quickly forgotten. We do notice a very wide range of marketing messages – special offers, promotions, posters, stickers, colour cues etc. – and these may influence our behaviour, but we rarely remember these influences because the conscious mind treats them as unimportant. On a related theme, Paco Underhill (2000) has suggested that brand choice is often made in store, at the point of sale, rather than planned in advance. Products may be purchased on impulse, through habit, or influenced by in-store promotions or sales activity, rather than through pre-planned and clearly motivated processes.

Thus, researchers have a situation in which one of the key influences on brand choice – in-store promotions and point of sale materials – is difficult to research through conventional interviews because people rarely remember them retrospectively. Indeed, various studies have shown that consumers frequently underestimate the influence of promotions and special offers, either because they do not recall being influenced, or because they do not want to be seen as the kind of person whose choice is swayed by such apparent trivia. In these cases, observation can be the only way to get a true picture of the range of factors that influence purchase decisions. National Opinion Polls in London have conducted various studies where fixed cameras are placed in supermarket aisles. Shoppers are filmed making purchases and interviewed afterwards. They may also be shown the video of their shopping behaviour and asked to discuss the reasons for their choices with the researcher. This method revealed that shoppers were in fact influenced by price promotions and in-store signs, although they often denied this until they saw the video of their own behaviour. As Kathryn Hall (2000) of NOP says:

> If you interviewed them in a group or a depth interview outside the store, they would say 'Oh I know exactly what I want, I know exactly where it is, I know exactly what I am doing.' But when you watch them in the shop and you get them to watch their own behaviour they will say 'Oh I wasn't even aware that I was in that aisle, I was on complete auto pilot.' They don't realise what they are doing half the time. And they don't realise how much they are influenced by little things like colour and shapes. Sometimes they would not even remember a brand, they'd just remember the shape of the jar.

Observation at the point of sale can also demonstrate what might prevent a consumer from purchasing a particular product or brand, and how the brand owner can act upon this. NOP's research, for example, found that shoppers in a particular supermarket associated certain colours with price offers, and therefore when faced with two brands they often chose the one with the coloured sign nearest to it.

> If they had to choose between one product and another product, people would deny that the sign had influenced them. But when you actually had them on video tape and you watched where they were looking, what they were doing at that time, it became very clear that they were just automatically reaching for the one with the sign above it. And then they would look at the one next to it, and the sign did have an influence on behaviour. But it was very difficult to get people to admit that.

Thus, although people might not be aware of the influence of point of sale materials, the use of observational methods can demonstrate that they are important, and can therefore give marketers better guidance on in-store promotions than interviews alone.

Impulse purchases are another area it is hard to research through conventional methods alone. By definition, if someone purchases a product on impulse, this means they did not intend to buy it when they started their shopping trip. It is therefore likely to be difficult for them to tell researchers why they bought a particular product, especially if asked to do so some time after the event. Chandler and Evans (2000: 5) observed people's behaviour in convenience stores, garage shops and off licences, making detailed records of exactly what people did and how they acted when in the shop. They describe people's behaviour when shopping on impulse as:

... a million miles away from the world of reasoned decision, of attitudinal shift, of shopping lists and so on. This is a world in which most behaviour is so trivial and unimportant that it doesn't warrant thought as we know it ... This is a world in which layout, display, packaging, flashes and promotions, assist or hinder the consumer's low key path. (i.e. the consumer does not pay active attention to these stimuli).

They emphasise the 'automatic' behaviour which people appear to adopt, and the low level of involvement in the actual purchase process, which is influenced by any number of minor point of sale cues. However, these minor cues can swing the consumer one way or another when they are wavering about what to buy, and observation can demonstrate the real importance of these promotions, whilst they tend to be understated in group discussions and interviews.

Habitual Action

As the above discussion makes clear, a lot of purchasing behaviour is less rational and premeditated than it appears. Whilst people can put together sensible narratives of the motivations behind particular purchases in groups and interviews, this does not necessarily reflect what is happening when people buy. As discussed in Chapter 1, much of human behaviour is conducted according to routines and habitual actions that rarely rise to the level of conscious thought. This area comprises routines that we carry out every day, often several times a day, without thinking consciously about what we are doing. Indeed, recent thinking in both neuroscience (Damasio 1994) and sociological theory (Bloch 1991; Bourdieu 1980; Johnson 1987) suggests that our ability to carry out these actions is not contained within the conscious mind, but rather at the level of 'embodied understanding'. We can drive our car to work, make a cup of tea, negotiate the concourse at Waterloo Station, shave or shower not because we think these things through every time we do them, but rather because our brains have developed neurological short-cuts which allow us to process the necessary information without involving the conscious mind. And these short-cuts are re-activated by the bodily reality of carrying out the action, not by active thought. What this means for research is that the amount of information which can be gained about these habitual, repeated actions through conventional questioning (i.e. the conscious mind) is limited. To explore these sorts of activity, the respondent needs to act them out in order to re-evoke the feelings associated with the activities, and this again implies an observational approach will be most useful.

To use a practical example, if a researcher wants to explore how someone feels when they drive their car to work, asking them to describe the feelings in a group will only get so much information. In order to get beyond what the rational mind can remember, the researcher should ideally accompany the respondent on the drive, perhaps video the experience, and then ask the respondent to describe their own feelings at each point. Similarly,

Pyke and Gordon conducted in home observations of women cleaning their toilets, and compared this with the data they gained from group discussions and accompanied shopping. They found that the ethnographic work gave them a particularly useful insight into the feelings associated with toilet cleaning, as the act of cleaning the toilet appeared to evoke feelings which discussion alone did not. If full-scale observation is not possible, these methods can be adapted for use in conventional groups. Collier (1993) suggests that researchers should encourage consumers to re-enact the behaviours being explored in groups, in order to access feelings and thoughts which are not available from discussion alone. Thus, if one is researching airline travel in a group discussion, it might be useful to re-arrange the chairs into rows for part of the group, to help people imagine themselves in a plane.

Packaging

The influence of packaging is also an important topic for observational research. Whilst it is possible to research pack design in group discussions or interviews, the way the pack performs in the retail context can only be fully assessed in-store. The relationship of the pack to other products in the category, the way it sits on the shelf, whether it attracts attention, can all be better assessed in the actual retail context. For example, Jack and Homans (2000) quote a case study in which a cosmetics brand was re-launched with new packaging and supporting advertising. The marketing promotions had researched well, but sales were disappointing. Observations in store quickly revealed that whilst the packaging was well received in group discussions, 'in the competitive context it was simply lost among other brands which seemed to "shout louder" at the point of sale' (2000: 9). Anniki Sommerville of Flamingo relates a similar example from the drinks market. When young people are at a crowded bar or nightclub buying drinks, brands need to be easily identifiable, because the decision on what to order has to be taken very quickly if you want to get served.

> Bars are very crowded and busy and you have to make a decision very quickly. So simple things like packaging are really, really important. When you have something on the table [in a group discussion], it might look quite impressive, but what does it look like when it's behind 70 other different drinks? If you've got to make a decision in 10 seconds and you've got 50 people pushing you along, you'd better be able to identify the brand. That is something that we wouldn't have learned if we were in a group context.

Thus, conventional group discussions could actually be misleading if used in isolation when assessing packs and point of sale displays. It is only when observing purchasing behaviour in context that a full understanding of their influence and likely performance in the real world can be gained.

Product Use

Finally, observational methods are also frequently employed to explore how products are used in the real world. Focusing on the details of product use can identify problems with existing products, potential improvements, unstated needs and new product opportunities. The way that people handle products and use them in group discussions or interviews is likely to differ from how the products would be used in the home or workplace, and therefore *in situ* observations can be very helpful.

For fast moving consumer goods – household cleaners, basic food products etc. – it can be very useful to see exactly what people do with the product once they get it home. An understanding of where the product is stored, what other brands are stored next to it, and how easy it is for the consumer to access can all be important in explaining sales patterns and consumer perceptions. For example, a product that is stored at the back of a cupboard is likely to be used less frequently than one which is stored in the fridge, so a manufacturer may want to encourage consumers to refrigerate their product.

In the technology field, it is common to observe how products are used by consumers in the product development phase, and there are some companies which specialise in 'usability testing'. This can reveal the reasons why products that appear technologically well designed may not work well in the real world, or may suffer from high levels of breakdown due to inappropriate uses. For example, the product innovation consultancy PDD were asked to redesign a gas detector for use by workmen who cleaned underground services including sewers. The detectors were designed to be worn on the jackets of the workmen, and emitted a warning sound if gas levels become too high. The manufacturers found that the detectors were frequently being returned due to water damage, though there was no obvious reason why they should fall in water. When PDD conducted some observations to see how the product was being used, they found that the workmen were tying the detector onto a piece of string and lowering it into the sewer to assess gas levels before actually going in, with the result that the detectors frequently hit the water at the bottom!

Design consultancy IDEO conduct observational research on most, if not all, of their design projects. Their head of human factors tells the story of how she worked on the ticket barriers for the London Underground, conducting observational research with various prototypes to identify the optimum height for the ticket slot. Clearly, it was important that commuters should be able to get their tickets into the slot first time, to avoid delays. From their observations, they determined that although height was important, it was at least as important to give the commuter a large 'target' to aim for with their ticket. They therefore concluded that rather than trying to design a larger slot, they would provide people with a larger target. In the final design, although the slot is still small, it is contained within a larger recessed area outlined in yellow on the actual barriers.

Bill Pegram gives another example from the personal computer market. Pegram Walters were asked by their American client to conduct research looking at the European market for computer peripherals – speakers, gaming devices etc. – and as part of the project they conducted in-home interviews where they observed how and where computers were used. This revealed immediately that the peripherals were designed with large American houses in mind. They would not fit easily into the more cramped European homes, where computers are often stuck in a corner or in a small spare room.

Finally, there are many examples of observational research showing that products may be used in ways that were not expected nor intended by the designers, although they may offer ideas for new developments. For example, BT conducted a large study looking at how people used the Internet, which included filming and tracking of Internet use among a small sample of consumers, as well as a large quantitative survey. They found that a surprising number of people failed to bookmark their favourite sites, but rather located the site via another site which functioned as a 'gateway'. This site might have an easier name to remember, or provide access to a range of other sites. They also found that whilst high Internet users estimated they visited around thirty sites a month, tracking their use showed that in fact they visited nearer to 1,400. However, in most cases they were just 'passing through' rather than actually using the site.

Other work conducted by BT revealed how people use direct mail, rather than how they claim they do. From their in-home observations they developed the concept of the 'nerve centre', a physical location in the house where things that need to be 'dealt with' are placed. It may be drawer, a fruit bowl, or a table. Direct mail which might be of some interest, but on which a decision has not been made, may be placed in the 'nerve centre' until the individual has the chance to go through it and decide on a course of action. In this context, the direct mail serves as a reminder to do something, and keeping a mailing does not indicate an intention to act upon that particular offer. Indeed, receiving a piece of direct mail about, say, credit cards, might prompt people to look for other credit card offers, resulting in the consumer buying a competitor product.

Thus, as well as providing insight into the wider social context, observation can also tell us about the micro-level detail of social interactions and product use. It can reveal influences people do not remember, or actions they are not aware of themselves. It can help access those influences which the brain deals with at the level of low involvement processing, but which may be decisive in determining brand choice at the point of sale. And it is therefore an important component in any research which aims to explore the purchase process.

Before moving on to discuss the more pragmatic issue of field tactics, we need to address one of the most vexed issues within observational research: the extent to which the fact of being observed may alter the behaviour of respondents, and therefore reduce the validity of the research.

THE OBSERVER EFFECT

Observation is sometimes seen as the nearest researchers can get to the 'real truth' – what people actually do, as opposed to what they claim or even may believe they do. However, there is considerable debate on the extent to which being observed may alter the behaviour that is the topic of the research – the so-called 'observer effect'. If people know they are being observed and change their behaviour as a result, the argument runs, this may invalidate the findings of the research. This has led some (e.g. Stafford and Stafford 1993) to argue for a greater use of covert methods – hidden cameras and microphones – in commercial research, in order to overcome the possible impact of the 'observer effect'. We shall discuss below the theoretical and practical issues involved in this debate, and suggest how commercial researchers can address them.

The first point to make is that it is inevitable that observation will affect behaviour in some way – the question is how great this effect is, and whether it is relevant to the research topic. Many of the studies quoted by Stafford and Stafford come from the field of organisational research, which is frequently concerned with improving the productivity of sales forces or production lines. In this context, it is not surprising that if factory workers are told they are being researched in order to evaluate their productivity, the fact of being observed may increase productivity! Indeed, commercial researchers would usually address this issue via 'mystery shopping', where researchers play the role of customers in order to provide feedback on how staff treat them. In these cases, staff would usually be told that mystery shopping was being used by the company, but the researcher would not identify themselves to the individual staff member(s). This would avoid the staff changing their behaviour and reducing the validity of the research findings.

However, there are many commercial research subjects where the observer effect is likely to be of limited relevance to the topic under exploration. In Gordon and Pike's study of toilet cleaning, for example, it is likely that some respondents may have cleaned their toilets more thoroughly than usual because the researchers were present. However, the researchers were interested in the *manner* in which the toilet was cleaned and the feelings this evoked, not how *thoroughly* it was cleaned, so this effect did not reduce the validity of their findings. Similarly, in observations that focus on product use and design, consumers might tidy their front room before the researcher's arrival, but they are unlikely to purchase new products or use their existing products in a different way. Thus, there clearly is an observer effect, but the effect is not relevant to the research topic.

Also, the 'observer effect' itself can be integrated into the analysis of the data – indeed, it can be seen as part of the data, revealing cultural norms and socially accepted behaviours within particular product fields. Gordon and Pike commented that 'several women felt uncomfortable being interviewed and videoed cleaning their toilets' and some told the researchers they felt they were being 'judged'. Further exploration led respondents to realise that they had never been shown how to clean the toilet, and therefore felt uncertain whether they were 'doing it right' or not. This insight could be valuable for a client in positioning a new cleaning product, for example, offering suggestions as to how best to clean the toilet or reassurance that consumers were indeed 'doing it right'. In longer-term ethnography, work conducted by the author among working-class young men suggested that they sometimes exaggerated their involvement in street conflicts in the presence of the researcher. However, by exploring this issue with the young men, it became clear that involvement in fighting was a key aspect of their sense of masculine identity. This in turn led to a greater exploration of how young men act out masculine identities for other audiences, such as rival groups, and enhanced rather than reduced the insights gained.

So, the observer effect may not always be relevant to the research topic, and can sometimes lead to new insights. However, in some instances the effect will indeed be potentially detrimental to the research. Frequently, this will be in precisely those areas where observational research is most likely to be used, that is, areas where there is a strong social pressure in interviews to 'say the right thing'. Studies of how thoroughly people clean, or how fast they drive, how much they drink, whether they give in to children's requests for unhealthy snacks – all these are likely to be subject to observer effects which might invalidate the research findings. There are essentially two approaches to this dilemma:

- Conduct **covert research**, i.e., do not inform people that the research is taking place.
- Attempt to **minimise the observer effect** through specific research strategies.

Covert research may be the only way to get valid data on some issues – for example, the effectiveness of a particular point of sale display, or the length of time people spend in a particular supermarket aisle. In this context, informing people that the research was taking place might change their behaviour in ways that invalidated the research. The Market Research Society Code of Conduct in the United Kingdom states that people must be informed if observational research methods are being used, unless the research occurs in a 'public place', and a supermarket would probably count as such. For example, although Paco Underhill (2000) does not describe his methods in detail, it seems that much of his work would be conducted on a purely observational basis – tracking people through shops without informing them that the research was taking place. Stafford and Stafford (1993) argue that covert observation is justifiable on a much wider scale, on the grounds that the respondents come to no harm as a result of taking part, and the data could not be effectively gained if they were informed about the research. In addition, there are many research contexts in which it would be simply impossible to gain informed consent in any meaningful fashion. In a crowded bar, a night-club, or a busy supermarket on a Saturday morning, it would not be possible to inform everyone there that research was taking place.

However, there is probably a limited range of environments which are commonly agreed to be so public that no form of consent is necessary for research – supermarkets, town squares and shopping centres might be uncontroversial, but what of pubs, bars, restaurants, public offices, hospital waiting rooms, or libraries? It is by no means certain that the general public would be completely at ease with the idea of being video-recorded for research purposes without being informed in all of these contexts. A general belief that researchers use covert methods could, in the long term, reduce the public's trust in market research and also lead to a confusion between research and other forms of video observation, such as security cameras and journalistic work.

In addition, there are many contexts in which covert observation is either impossible, or very difficult. For example, it might be possible for a researcher to insinuate him or herself among a group of young people in a bar and 'tag along' with them for an evening without disclosing their research agenda. However, it would be very difficult in practice to main-tain such a role, the sample achieved and data gathered would be very 'hit and miss', and the process would almost certainly require the researcher to deceive the 'respondents' about their identity and background. The ethical and practical problems involved in such an approach comprise a compelling argument for a more overt form of observation. Similarly, in-home observations clearly cannot be carried out without the respondents' consent.

Thus, for the majority of commercial research projects, completely covert research will not be an option. If the researcher is worried about the observer effect, he or she will need to take steps to minimise its impact, and there are various means of doing this.

- **Spending a longer period with respondents** to reduce the impact of the observer effect on behaviour. This can be via repeated visits, either on consecutive days or at regular intervals. Respondents may be able to change their behaviour for a day or two, but if the researcher is with them for a week or even longer, they usually revert to their normal behaviours. Siamack Salari says that when he visits households, he notices a change over time: on the first visit, the house is very tidy and the participants try hard to help, but as time goes on the house seems to revert to normal and people stop asking him 'is this interesting to you?'
- **Using fixed cameras** in the home, or **giving the respondents the camera**. Salari has conducted research on Internet use where fixed cameras were placed on top of the computer in respondents' homes,

and respondents were asked to turn it on whenever they used the computer. If respondents themselves have control over the technology, this again can reduce their desire to change their behaviour – they can simply switch the camera off if they do not want to be recorded.

- **Comparing different sources of data:** for example, comparing what someone does in a supermarket with what is in their cupboard at home, with what they say in an interview. Any differences can then be explored with the respondent, and the reasons uncovered.
- **Observing people in different social contexts.** If observing a family activity, it can be helpful to visit when only one family member is present, and then also observe the same behaviour when other members are present. Other people who know the respondent well can then assess whether the behaviour is typical or unusual. Again, Siamack Salari tells the story of a respondent whose wife pointed out that he used a teaspoon to take coffee from the jar only when Siamack was present. When the researcher was absent, he simply shook the coffee straight from the jar into his cup!
- **Playing back observations.** If video observation is being used, tapes can be played back to the respondent for their comments. The researcher can then take the opportunity to ask both the respondent and other family members if the behaviour observed is what they normally do, or if it is unusual in any way. In some cases, an explicit request to respond honestly – 'We know people sometimes feel pressured to clean more thoroughly because we are researching the topic. Is this really how you clean ever day?' – can encourage the respondent to evaluate the typicality of their own behaviour.
- **Concealing the exact topic of the research.** As with group discussions and interviews, there are cases where to reveal the exact topic of the research might bias people's responses, and in these cases a general explanation can be given. For example, when Flamingo do observations among young people in bars, they do not usually reveal which brand they are focusing on. Similarly, a project that focused on how thoroughly people cleaned their kitchens might be described as focusing on household routines or tasks; or a project focusing on speeding in cars might be described as being about people's attitudes to their cars. In effect, this is a milder form of covert research, where the respondent is informed that research is taking place, but is not told exactly what the research is about.

Thus, completely covert observation is rarely an option for commercial researchers; both ethically and pragmatically, they will usually have to inform the participants that the research is taking place. The key issue for the commercial researcher is whether any observer effect is relevant to the behaviour being explored, and if it is, how the researcher can account for it in analysis, and minimise its detrimental effect on the data.

FIELD TACTICS

Thus far, we have discussed the theoretical issues involved in conducting observational research and ethnography, and the research topics for which these methods are particularly well adapted. The remainder of this chapter outlines how these methods are used in the field and how commercial qualitative researchers may need to adapt their practice if they are carrying out ethnographic studies.

Commercial researchers have adapted ethnographic and observational methods in a variety of ways, often combining them with interviews or group discussions, or integrating ethnographic approaches into more conventional methods. Before discussing the practical implications of using ethnographic methods, it is worth while outlining the main examples of these approaches as used by commercial researchers.

- **'Nights out':** spending an evening with a group of consumers, usually young people, and then convening a group a week later to discuss behaviour.
- **'Day in the life':** shadowing someone for a day to observe a specific activity and how it fits into their lives, e.g., their use of a car, or of a personal computer.
- **In-home interviewing:** in-depth interviews are usually conducted in home, and therefore can often be enhanced by adding an observational component. For example, research on eating habits can be combined with a look in the respondent's fridge, or research on fashion can involve going through favourite outfits with the respondent and taking photographs.
- **Enhanced accompanied shopping:** meeting the consumer before they go shopping, going to the supermarket with them, doing the shopping, coming home with them and watching them unpack the shopping and put things away. This can be combined with pre and post interviews to ensure that the consumer's attitudes as well as behaviour are explored.
- **'Intercept interviews'** at the point of sale: observing the consumer in retail outlets and then inviting them to be interviewed to discuss their shopping behaviour.
- **Ethnographic immersion:** spending longer periods of time with consumers without focusing on specific activities, e.g. spending a week with a consumer and watching all their activities, usually video recording them.
- Using various pre-tasks to **turn the respondent into an amateur ethnographer.** Prior to attending a group discussion or interview, they can be asked to photograph important aspects of their lives, keep a diary of the behaviour being explored, make audio recordings of particular occasions or experiences. The consumer can bring these ethnographic

materials to the interview and use them as the basis for discussion. Although this is not observation in the strictest sense, it is a good and cost-effective alternative and may also reduce the observer effect, as the respondent is in control of the technology.

These are probably the most commonly used observational methods in commercial research. Although they have much in common with conventional qualitative methods, there are aspects of research which may need to be altered if ethnographic research is being conducted, and these are discussed in the final section of this chapter:

Sample Design and Recruitment

One of the most common questions asked of commercial researchers is how many observations need to be carried out. What size of sample is required for the data to be sufficiently reliable and robust? How far can one generalise from observational data? And how can one be sure that the examples observed – of people washing, cooking, eating, or whatever – are representative of all the cases of these activities? The optimum sample design and size will clearly depend on the scope and the aims of the study. Also, and perhaps more importantly, it will depend on whether observation is the main method used, or whether it is in addition to other qualitative or quantitative research methods.

Observation is rarely the only method used in a commercial qualitative study, but Siamack Salari and Hy Mariampolski do carry out entirely observational work for their clients. Mariampolski (1997) suggests that in such studies, the criteria for guiding the sample design are the same as for any qualitative study.

- **Comprehensiveness:** can the researcher be sure to have observed all the examples of the behaviour being studied?
- **Comparability:** has the researcher observed a sufficient number of examples to be able to compare key sub-groups, such as older or younger respondents, or men and women?

As Mariampolski points out, these criteria are unlikely to be met with fewer than 15 observations if the activity is a fairly widespread one, i.e., if the sample is a cross-section of the general public. Salari's work usually includes around 25 families per project, suggesting that as a rule of thumb somewhere between 15 and 25 observations may be a sensible sample size (depending on objectives and the diversity of the target audience, of course).

However, most commercial research studies use ethnographic methods as an add-on to conventional research methods, or to generate hypotheses that can be subject to testing in quantitative research. In these cases, the observational data may be used to contextualise or to illustrate the main findings, and here a smaller range of observations will suffice. For example, in Pegram Walters' study of the European home computer market referred to above, the researchers conducted 12 groups across three countries and also did two in-home ethnographic interviews in each country. In this case, the video data from the ethnographic interviews was used to add impact to the presentation and contextualise the data from the groups. Similarly, the first BT Street study included five households who were visited several times over a period of six weeks, and the hypotheses generated from this detailed observation were then tested in quantitative research, resulting in the concept of the nerve centre discussed above. When Flamingo do research among young people on drinking behaviour, they usually accompany the respondents on a night out, and then convene a group a week later to discuss the event. This would mean that each observational session would have a corresponding group discussion, resulting in a sample size such as four groups and four observational sessions.

The principles of recruitment to ethnographic studies are the same as for any qualitative project, although the practicalities may differ somewhat. Observational methods demand greater commitment from participants than group discussions or interviews – the researcher enters the participants' life, whether for a few hours or several months. This raises the issue of who would be willing to take part in such studies, and how to ensure that the right participants are recruited and the wrong ones are not. Those who are willing to take part may be atypical of the general public – either they may see the research as a chance to enhance their social lives, or they may be 'professional respondents' who are very familiar with research processes. Genuine 'ordinary people', on the other hand, may be reluctant to let a stranger into their house to video their day-to-day lives.

There are various approaches which can be taken to address this issue. Mariampolski (1997) suggests that participants for observational research studies need more information and reassurance about the research: who will be coming to their house, what will happen to the data, and how they will be treated? Siamack Salari prefers to avoid using fieldwork agencies, instead placing advertisements in the local press, whilst researchers at Flamingo prefer to use informal networks. And Mrazek, Dray and Dyer (1995) recruited respondents for a three-country study of home computer use via cold calling, press adverts and re-contacting respondents from previous group discussions. And both Siamack Salari and Kirsty Fuller have emphasised the importance of careful screening and selection procedures for observational studies. Fuller recommends that the research executive should phone each respondent personally to ensure that they meet the criteria, whilst Salari recommends visiting potential respondents in their homes before finalising their recruitment to longer observational research. Doing this prior to the main fieldwork can also help ensure the personal safety of the researcher, which again is more of an issue in ethnographic than in conventional qualitative research.

Thus, recruitment for observational research projects may require different approaches from conventional qualitative research, and is likely to require more involvement and management from the research agency if it is to successfully access the right participants.

Defining the Topic

In sociological and anthropological research, ethnographic methods often have a very wide focus. The researcher immerses him or herself within the total culture of a group of people and tries to pay attention to everything that is happening – the language used, the social relations established, the different behaviours in different contexts, gender roles, cultural values and religious ideology. Later in the fieldwork, the researcher might choose to focus down on a particular aspect of the culture under study, but the precise topic is rarely defined in advance.

Commercial ethnographic studies, however, need a more precisely defined topic if they are to gather useful and relevant data for the client. Indeed, there appears to be a move away from very broad studies, towards more specific and manageable topics. This allows the researcher to generate more relevant and productive data for the client, and to avoid the rather 'hit and miss' nature of pure observation, in which it is possible to spend several days with a participant and gather very little valuable data. Bill Parton, Research Manager of Kraft Foods, has commissioned observational research on food consumption in the home as part of a joint project with other non-competitive manufacturers. He described the results as 'absolutely fascinating', but points out that it can be difficult to gain relevant marketing insights from very general observational studies. He says the key learning from his work in this field is 'you have to be pretty damn focused' in your objectives in order to be sure of gathering relevant data.

Field Relations

The relationship between the researcher and participants is a key issue in all qualitative research, but in ethnographic studies it has a particular importance. This is because the researcher becomes more involved in the respondents' lives, spends longer with them, and often observes and accompanies them carrying out tasks and activities. The role of the researchers within these different contexts is not always clear, and indeed respondents and researchers may have differing expectations. The respondent may see the researcher as a special guest, and may purchase different food or drink to entertain their guest. In the field of technology, the researcher may be seen as an expert source of advice and authority, and the respondent may feel the need to gain the researcher's approval or ask their opinion. And in longer-term studies, the researcher can become a temporary friend, with the respondent enjoying their company on a social level.

Clearly, there is a balance to be struck between being friendly and encouraging the respondent to relax, and maintaining a certain professional neutrality and distance. Whilst emphasising the need to be friendly and non-threatening, Mariampolski suggests that it is best to maintain a professional researcher's role, and not to step outside this unless there is a compelling reason to do so. For example, if the respondent is doing something dangerous or damaging to their health, the researcher should inform them, but as a general rule the researcher should maintain a professional neutrality.

Siamack Salari, on the other hand, emphasises the need to be completely open and honest with participants. He suggests that the researchers should share aspects of their personal and family life with the respondents, and that the relationship between researcher and respondent should be one of reciprocal revelation. He also suggests it is important to maintain contact with respondents after the research has finished, and that the researcher should make themselves available to respondents as far as possible during the research process.

It seems that there are two issues here. First, there is the question of whether the researcher may bias or alter the respondent's behaviour if they reveal too much about themselves. In this case, it does seem sensible to follow Mariampolski's advice and to avoid interfering with or calling into question respondent's natural behaviour. This does not mean the researcher cannot share aspects of their own life – whether they are planning a holiday, or what films they have seen recently. Indeed, if a researcher were to spend a week following someone around without ever revealing anything about themselves, they would be unlikely to develop much of a rapport with the respondent. However, it does mean that they should avoid revealing their own preferences or behaviour about the research topic.

The second issue relates to the professional and personal ethics of the researcher: for example, if a respondent wants to maintain contact with the researcher after the project is finished what is the correct response? In some cases, researchers may value continuing contact with respondents – they can try out new ideas or contact them about future projects. But in other cases the respondent may simply want to be the researcher's friend, on a purely social basis. Whilst individual researchers may make their own decisions in each case, it seems undesirable that continuing friendship should be established as a norm or a precedent in research. The relationship between researcher and respondent is primarily a professional one, and it is important that this should be clear from the outset to avoid inappropriate expectations being generated. That does not mean that the relationship cannot also be friendly and mutually enjoyable. However, it does mean that when the project is finished and the researcher leaves the field, the respondent should not feel that they have been abandoned by a new friend.

Recording, Analysing and Interpreting the Data

Qualitative interviews and group discussions are usually audio-recorded, and the tape or transcripts are the main analytical resource. For observational or ethnographic research, video recording is increasingly the norm, as this provides a complete and accurate record of the behaviour being observed. In some cases, this video recording will be treated as data and will be subject to analysis, but in others it can be used mainly to illustrate the findings from more conventional qualitative research methods. In particular, for studies that focus on product use, design or research at the point of sale, video recordings are often very helpful both as analysis tools and also to communicate the results to designers or marketers.

When the research is focusing on a particular occasion, such as a night out, or a Saturday afternoon shopping, video recording can get in the way, provoking forms of behaviour that would not otherwise occur, and inhibiting the researcher's interaction with the participants. In these cases, the researcher will need to take 'fieldnotes', ideally at the time of the observation, but if this is not possible, then very soon afterwards. These notes serve two purposes: first, they form a descriptive record of what was observed, in as much detail as possible; and secondly, they give the researcher the opportunity to record their initial thoughts – the first level of analysis and interpretation. For some studies it can be helpful to have an observation schedule, in order to focus the researcher on the key issues and to ensure a degree of comparability between different observations.

If the fieldwork is video-recorded, observational research can generate a huge amount of data which can be very difficult to analyse and interpret. For example, if a study covers 15 households, each of which is observed on two separate occasions for an afternoon, that could generate up to 90 hours of video tape. Going through all this data is clearly an onerous task, and it is probably only when the research topic is clearly focused that it can be achieved within a manageable timescale. Also, observational data lends itself to re-analysis, because there is often a lot of data gathered that is not relevant to the topic in hand, but which may be relevant to another topic that emerges in future. Re-analysis of existing qualitative data is not common in commercial research, but it could save time and money for clients.

Analysis and interpretation are rarely discussed in commercial market research and this is particularly true of observational data. Most of the published papers focus on how to do observational research, the additional insights which can be gained, and issues such as reliability and objectivity. They rarely discuss the approaches, methods or techniques which can assist in making sense of observational data.

In part, this may be because observational data is frequently used for illustrative purposes – effectively, it is there to 'bring the consumer to life', but it is not the primary source of data. Also, observational data can appear self-explanatory, not requiring analysis or interpretation. It makes an immediate and vivid impact on clients, and it can seem irrefutable – seeing is believing. This is a major strength of observational work, but it is also a real danger. Whilst it may appear to be the 'unmediated truth', analysis and interpretation is just as important for observational data as for conventional research methods. Without attention to analysis, researchers may misinterpret the data and misinform their clients. They may have chosen to observe the wrong behaviour in the wrong place, or the examples chosen may not be typical of behaviour in the target audience, or they may not have observed a sufficient number of cases. In pure observation, researchers may wrongly assume they understand the consumer's motivations and attitudes from their behaviour. Showing a video and commenting on it does not constitute observational research. The researcher needs to be able to explain and account for the behaviour being explored – to look at ordinary, everyday behaviour and see something that other people do not. As Siamack Salari explains: 'I wanted to look at specifically ordinary things and events and then try to pull out extraordinary things, and that's very hard to do.' This means that the observational researcher needs to be sensitive to issues such as the following.

- The **context of the behaviour** being observed. What is the location and what physical constraints does this place on behaviour? Who else is present and absent, how does this compare to similar behaviour observed in other contexts? What else is happening at the same time?
- **Social patterns of interaction.** Who is interacting with whom, how is this interaction taking place, what are the roles of verbal and non-verbal communications?
- The **rituals and routines** of every day life. What are people doing without thinking, or with little active thought?
- The **taken-for-granted assumptions** within particular social groups or contexts. What is nobody questioning? What assumptions need to be held for this behaviour to make sense?
- The **functions of the activity** being observed. What is its practical role? What is its symbolic role?
- The **emotional tone** of the activity. How do people feel during the behaviour observed?

By adopting a holistic approach to the analysis of observational data, researchers can explain what is happening in a way that transcends mere commentary and reveals insights that are not apparent to others viewing the same behaviour. Siamack Salari describes the analysis of observational data thus:

Instead of focusing on an activity or an event, like it's a discrete event, it's being able to put it into an overall picture, to see how it fits in. It puts it into context and it totally changes the way that you think about your product ... Observational research isn't about discovery, it's discovering what you've already known. That's what an insight is. That's why we try to go for ordinary events and activities, to try and pull out insights. There's nothing interesting about something extraordinary.

Thus, the practical issues that arise in conducting observational research are the same as those that arise in conventional qualitative market research. However, the fact that the fieldwork can be longer term and involve a wider range of tasks means that we need to adapt our recruitment and fieldwork methods to account for this, and pay particular attention to the relationship between the respondent and the researcher. Observational studies can also generate a huge amount of data, and therefore it is important to have a focused research question and clear analysis strategy.

CONSUMER CONNECTION PROGRAMMES

Before concluding, we need to cover one final use of observational and ethnographic methods which has grown in popularity recently – Consumer Connection programmes. In the UK there is a growing tendency for clients to attend group discussions, and this has been the norm in the USA for some time. This relates to clients' desire to experience the fieldwork for themselves, rather than rely on the researchers' reporting of the results. This is especially true of observational studies, where the clients and researchers sometimes work together as a team during field-work, rather than in a supplier–purchaser relationship (Denny 1995; Mrazek et al. 1995; Trevaskis 2000). Indeed, Denny believes there are great benefits in clients participating in ethnographic research, as they gain better and deeper insights from actually being present.

It is not surprising, therefore, that many companies are now engaging in direct contact with consumers rather than relying wholly on conventional, arm's length research methods. The Market Research Society Newsletter of October 2000 described the use of Consumer Connection programmes by companies including Van Den Bergh (now Unilever Bestfoods), Kraft Foods, ASDA, Ford and Microsoft, among others. The programmes are often run by research agencies, and members of the client company are given the opportunity to engage in various activities with consumers. Typical activities might be a shopping trip, an evening watching dinner being prepared, or simply a chat to discuss a new product idea. The programmes are not necessarily restricted to marketing personnel, and indeed some clients have suggested that the wider the involvement is spread, the better the effect within the organisation. Clients are usually given some basic training in listening and questioning skills by the research agency managing the programme, and also guidance on what to look out for when observing behaviour. Ideally, there should also be a debrief after each consumer contact session, allowing the attendee to consider what they have learnt, and what the implications are for their day-to-day work.

Most clients who use these methods say that they derive from the desire to 'get closer to consumers' – to understand people in a more intimate, meaningful and personal way, and to have a better insight into their lives, values and aspirations. Sometimes, such programmes are implemented because an organisation may feel it has lost touch with its customers and needs to take some radical action to avoid falling behind the competition.

Also, marketers are increasingly different from their consumers, in terms of their TV viewing, food consumption and leisure habits. Direct contact with consumers can help bridge this gap, giving marketers a more personal understanding of consumers, and making them feel they know, understand and respect them. It helps marketers relate to consumers as real human beings, rather than statistics or stereotypes, and makes them more enthusiastic about meeting the consumers' needs. Direct contact can also make clients feel more confident in their decision-making, give them an intuitive feeling for what will work and what will not, and therefore avoid going too far in developing unsuccessful ideas. Finally, clients also gain a deeper sense of commitment to their ideas if these are based on a direct, intuitive understanding of the consumer, and this can make it easier for them to argue their case within the organisation.

CONCLUSIONS

Observation and ethnography are long-established techniques which are central to anthropology and sociology. They have been used in commercial research for decades, but they have grown in popularity recently and can overcome some of the problems with interview data outlined in Chapter 1. Although limitations of time and money mean that full ethnographic studies are unlikely to become the norm in commercial market research, there are many ways in which an ethnographic approach can enhance the value of group discussions and interviews. By using more flexible recruitment methods, getting respondents to complete diaries or take photographs before the groups, conducting extended interviews in respondents' homes, filming them and asking them to comment on their own behaviour, or encouraging people to re-enact their behaviour in groups, the researcher can gather richer and more insightful data than through discussion alone.

However, the fact that observational data can be seen as self-explanatory, and is often visually very powerful, presents dangers for researchers or clients who would use it naïvely. Video footage is frequently used merely for illustrative purposes – 'to bring the consumer to life' – rather than being analysed as a primary source of data. Whilst this may have some value, it also undersells the potential of observational data to gain insights that are not accessible through interview methods. There is a risk that observational data may not be seen to require analysis in the way that other, more conventional data sources do – after all, seeing is believing. But this could result in unrepresentative findings, incorrect interpretations and misleading advice to clients. Thus, researchers need to draw on the strengths of these methods, but maintain the analytical rigour and professionalism which characterise more conventional methods.

KEY POINTS

- Observation and ethnography have long been used in sociology and anthropology, although they have only recently grown in popularity in commercial market research.
- Their main strength is that they are based on real behaviour rather than reports of claimed behaviour, and therefore allow researchers to overcome some of the problems associated with interview data.
- Ethnographic methods are suitable for target audiences who may be difficult to access via conventional methods – certain groups of young people, for example – and also for markets where there is a strong social pressure to conform, such as healthy eating or household cleaning.
- They can be very helpful to explore the social, cultural and physical contexts of purchasing and product use, putting individual brands or activities within a broader frame.
- They can also help in exploring the minutiae of daily rituals and routines, the influence of point of sale merchandising, and the details of product use which are rarely actively remembered.
- Particular attention needs to be paid to recruitment issues and relationships with respondents, as observational methods often require a longer-term involvement on the part of researcher and respondent.
- There is a danger that observational data can be seen as self-explanatory and therefore not requiring skilled interpretation and analysis. This is plainly wrong, and researchers need to ensure that they make this clear to their clients.

Research, Creativity and the Future

This chapter discusses how qualitative research techniques are used in processes of innovation and in understanding, predicting and shaping the future. First, the chapter outlines why innovation and 'futurology' have become key business themes, and discusses the limitations of conventional research approaches in this area. The discussion then moves on to outline how qualitative research has been adapted to assist in innovation and creative processes, suggesting that although qualitative researchers do have many relevant skills, the research 'mindset' can stifle creativity. Finally, the role of research in managing the future is considered, and how qualitative research skills can help organisations prepare for, and shape, the future.

'THE AGE OF UNCERTAINTY'

Innovation is probably one of the hottest corporate topics at the moment. Whilst in the past, companies might have thought it necessary to create new products or brands when the old ones were wearing out, now the trend is for continuous innovation as an integral part of corporate strategy. It is argued that things do not change once and then stabilise for a period of time but, rather, markets are in a state of continuous change and commercial companies need to build innovation into their ways of working rather than see it as an occasional, one-off event (Gibson 1998; Gordon 1999a; Holder and Young 1997). This continual desire for new products results in 'hyper-production', a condition seen by Jameson (1991) as typical of late capitalism.

There are many reasons for the raised profile of innovation within corporations, mostly relating to the condition of postmodernism discussed in Chapter 1.

- Markets change more quickly than they did in the past, requiring faster reactions from marketers.
- Technology is moving at a faster pace than ever before, meaning products which are state of the art today may be obsolete in two years' time.

- Many markets are now saturated with high-quality products, and therefore consumer choice may be made on the basis of minor differences or improvements.
- Consumers are inundated with advertising and marketing messages, and their attention will only be held by new, striking ideas.

These factors are particularly relevant for youth and fashion-driven markets, such as clothing, alcoholic drinks, leisure, media and technology. In these areas, the fear of being left behind by faster moving competitors is very real.

Linked to the theme of innovation is the question of the future, which is seen by many commentators as increasingly unpredictable. Traditional forecasting techniques have relied on looking at past trends, and extrapolating from these into the future. This is based on the following assumptions:

- There is good historical data about the subject.
- Present trends will continue into the future.
- There will be no major unpredictable events which change the situation.

Essentially, accurate forecasting relies on a linear relationship between the past and the future, where to predict the future all we need to do is analyse past trends and project these same patterns into the future. And indeed, in some cases this may work. For example, we can predict with a reasonable degree of accuracy the population of the country in ten years' time, because most of the people who will be alive have already been born, death rates can be estimated with reasonable accuracy – and we are unlikely to be hit by an asteroid (Local Government Association 2000). Quantitative researchers can predict response rates for surveys because they have conducted many similar surveys in the past, and there is no reason to think there will be massive and rapid change in public attitudes to market research.

However, increasingly, commercial markets are not thought to operate according to predictable and stable trends, and this makes forecasting difficult. For example, management guru Rowan Gibson suggests that 'the future will not be a continuation of the past. It will be series of discontinuities' (1998: 6). Indeed, many commercial markets now exhibit the following features:

- There is little historical data because technological advances make entirely new products possible.
- Markets are influenced by a complex web of global, regional and local factors. These factors are interdependent and cannot be predicted or incorporated into statistical models.
- Change is likely to be discontinuous rather than incremental, so there is no guarantee current trends will continue into the future.

Thus, in commercial markets where these conditions obtain, the value of predictions based on conventional research needs to be reconsidered. Research is based on the past: we ask people about things they have done, experiences they have had, how they behaved in the past. We look at historical data, trends in the market, and we frequently try to guess what those people will do in the future. And according to many commentators, whilst our suggestions are helpful in the short term, in the long term our predictions are of limited use. They argue that this is because we think in a linear fashion, whereas markets now operate according to the laws of chaos theory where 'one event may change those that follow in a wholly unpredictable, even devastating way' (Crichton, quoted in Gibson 1998). The point is not that we cannot learn from the past – clearly we can – but rather that assumptions we make about the relationship between the past and the future need to be re-thought.

In addition to the problem of research adopting backward-looking, linear models, the idea of relying on 'typical consumers' to judge new ideas and products can also be questioned (Holder and Young 1997). In the oversupplied markets within which many companies operate, consumers do not see themselves as having unmet needs, and may be cynical about minor innovations (Gordon 1999a). Consumers are inherently conservative and do not like changes to their favourite brands or products. They reject challenging creative ideas which 'break the mould', and they judge new ideas according to past experiences, rather than future possibilities. If marketers allow themselves to be guided by current consumer thinking, the argument runs, this would result in a range of very similar 'Me Too' products, neither good nor bad. Mark Earls (2001: 337) suggests that the 'rise of the bland Euro-car' is attributable at least in the part to an over-reliance on car clinics and the stifling influence of research.

Nevertheless, in spite of the problems with using qualitative research for predictive or creative purposes, it is important to maintain a sense of balance in the face of the sometimes overinflated claims of writers on this topic. Some of the literature on the subject gives the impression that we live in a world of complete chaos and uncertainty, where nothing is predictable, where the past offers no useful insights about the future, and we have no idea what markets or consumers will be doing from one day to the next (Gibson 1998; Holder and Young 1997; Wacker and Taylor 1999, quoted in Gordon 1999a). This is clearly an overstatement, and seems to be based on the assumption that because we cannot predict marketing outcomes with certainty, we cannot make any predictions at all.

A more sensible approach might be to ask what we can predict, and how certain we can be of our predictions. For example, it may be easier to predict short-term rather than long-term outcomes. We may be able to predict whether a piece of advertising copy will be understood by its target audience, but less able to predict whether it will prompt them to take action. And where there is a greater degree of uncertainty, we can still make educated guesses, or indicate what the range of likely outcomes is in any particular situation. For example, if an advertiser wants to know what sort of music teenagers will be listening to in six months' time so they can plan their campaign, we cannot tell them with certainty. We can analyse the emerging trends and make an educated guess about the most likely candidates, although we need to acknowledge the inherent uncertainty in such guesses.

Similarly, much of the criticism levelled against 'focus groups' in the context of advertising development seems more relevant to bad research than to qualitative methods *per se*. We do not ask respondents whether or not they 'like' adverts, or what they think the client should do. Rather, we gain their reactions and try to assess whether these meet the brief. Also, it is worth observing that creative ideas which are rejected on the basis of research may indeed be weak ideas, rather than creative gems crushed by the pedestrian researcher.

Nevertheless, hype and special pleading aside, there are real questions to be addressed in both these areas about the role and value of qualitative research. It is true that research is based on the past – how could it be otherwise? Also, the research mindset and the creative mindset do have different priorities, and it is legitimate to ask how far conventional research can help generate creative ideas.

This chapter will look at how qualitative researchers can facilitate innovation rather than suppress it, and at how we can help companies understand, predict and even shape the future, while acknowledging the uncertainty inherent in any prediction. The remainder of the chapter looks first at research and creativity and, secondly, at researching the future.

RESEARCH AND CREATIVITY

Qualitative research and creativity make uneasy bedfellows. Some qualitative research skills are highly conducive to facilitating creativity, but sometimes researchers' priorities and approaches seem to stifle it. For example, qualitative researchers are good at:

- Putting people at ease.
- Creating a relaxed environment.
- Managing social interaction.
- Thinking through analogies and metaphors.

All these skills are necessary to help people think creatively and to come up with new ideas. However, the researchers also have other priorities which work against creativity. For example, other factors generally agreed to promote creativity (Gordon 1999a; Mattimore 1994; Spenser and Wells 2000) include:

- Bringing together diverse viewpoints or conflicting perspectives.
- Producing a large number of sketchy ideas, rather than a few well-developed concepts.
- Suspending analytical faculties and allowing intuition and playfulness to take over.
- Not wasting time on debating or asking questions.
- Building on the ideas of others, rather than pointing out their deficiencies.

These are not usually the priorities of a qualitative researcher. In fact, the mindset of the researcher can be quite the opposite of the creative mindset. Researchers

- Want reliability and representativeness of data.
- Work with homogeneous groups and tend to seek a single 'story' in the data.
- Are analytical and value logical coherence in their findings.
- Ask questions and like to understand things fully before accepting them.
- Prefer verbal discussion to tasks and outcomes.

Thus, qualitative researchers possess a set of skills relevant to facilitating innovation, but their outlook, mindset and priorities can often inhibit creativity. In order to enhance creativity, researchers need to redirect their current skills and give themselves different goals. Rather than thinking 'How can we gather reliable information about this topic?', they need to ask 'What do we need to do to come up with creative solutions to this problem?' Wendy Gordon (1999a) has suggested that an eclectic approach – 'bricolage' – is required if researchers are to look to the future rather than the past. She suggests that rather than seeing themselves as rational researchers, qualitative researchers should conceptualise their activity as 'intelligent sleuthing'. Indeed, she suggests this activity should be termed 'pro-search', rather than 're-search', in order to indicate the focus on future possibilities.

Spenser and Wells (2000) have written a very useful paper on how qualitative research skills can be redirected to help facilitate, rather than stifle creativity. They suggest that there are some key changes that need to be made to conventional qualitative research in order to generate creative ideas.

- Recruit those who have something interesting to say, not necessarily the target market for the product.
- Move away from the standard group format.
- Shift from an 'information paradigm' to a 'task paradigm'.
- Bring together the clients and the consumers, rather than keeping them apart.
- Separate the processes of creation and evaluation of new ideas.

These are discussed in detail below.

Recruitment

Conventional research projects usually aim to recruit individuals who are in the target market for a product or advertisement, and who are in some way typical of the market. People who have a particular interest or specialist knowledge of the research topic are usually screened out in order to avoid influencing the other respondents.

However, for projects focusing on creativity one might adopt a different approach, speaking to people who have something interesting to say about a product or category, rather than those who use it. This might include, for example:

- People who are very interested in a particular product field, sometimes referred to as 'obsessives'.
- Experts, such as journalists, writers or academics.
- Professionals whose expertise is relevant, such as designers or artists.
- People whose relationship with a product or category has been disrupted or changed in some way, in order to give them a heightened awareness of activities which other people take for granted.

For example, when the innovation consultancy !What If? were looking for new ideas for a hair care product, their sample included:

- A man with dreadlocks
- A bald person
- A woman whose husband washed her hair for her every week
- A woman who changed her hair colour every week.

And when they were trying to understand people's relationships to mobility, they chose to interview people whose ability to move about had been restricted recently, such as people with broken legs or bad backs. Clearly, they were not looking for people who were typical of a target market in either of these examples, but rather for people whose perspective would be different from the norm and who might therefore have interesting new insights into the category or topic.

Logistics

The conventional structure of the group discussion – six to eight people, in a room, sitting down, for an hour and a half – may need to be changed. Larger groups may be better for bringing together a range of viewpoints and providing the opportunity for cross-fertilisation. For example, when Pegram Walters Associates were conducting research on the lifestyles of young people (in a project discussed below), they invited 50 young people to workshop sessions lasting a whole evening. During the course of the session, participants broke into smaller groups for particular tasks and periodically came together to see each other's ideas and spark off new thinking.

Different locations can allow people to be more relaxed, or to think in ways that they would not normally do. According to Spenser and Wells (2000), finding an appropriate venue is an important part of any idea generation project. Either the venue can be part of the stimulus – running a workshop on new designs for drinks packaging in a bar – or it can serve as a signal that something unusual is happening and give people licence to think more creatively. For example, when The Research Business International were doing a project on brand development for a media company, they hired a tall ship for a day-long workshop because they wanted a venue where people could feel relaxed and able to think 'out of the box'. After the research session they also took the clients and the participants out to dinner, so they could continue their discusson in an environment that was not the normal research context.

Longer sessions can also help, by removing the pressurised atmosphere that can exist in conventional 1½ hour groups. Although researchers tend to think we give people enough time, respondents can experience groups as rushed, with the researcher struggling to get through the stimulus materials. Workshops can last anything between half a day and three days, giving people enough time to come up with new ideas.

Moving about can also help people maintain their energy during sessions. Sitting down for 90 minutes is likely to make people feel tired, drowsy and lacking in energy, as blood flow and breathing slow down, less oxygen enters the brain and people become mentally less sharp. Encouraging people to get up, look at something in another room, walk around the locations – all these can help maintain people's energy levels, as well as providing alternative and informal opportunities to interact. For example, the simple device of displaying stimulus material as a 'gallery' during a group – hanging it around the room and asking respondents to 'tour' it – can elicit different responses from those gained while squashed on the sofa of a viewing facility!

From an 'Information Paradigm' to a 'Task Paradigm'

David Spenser has criticised qualitative researchers for operating within what he terms an 'information paradigm ... preoccupied with bringing "the findings" (whether "information" or "understanding") back from the consumer/market into the company' (Spenser and Wells 2000: 240). Lengthy verbal discussions are not the best way to arrive at new creative ideas, and indeed the rationality which such an approach generates can be antithetical to creative thinking. The experience of being 'talked out of a good idea' is something most people can relate to, and it may be that the group discussion format prompts this sort of negative response. Spenser suggests that we need to abandon the 'question and answer' format and replace it with a 'task-led' approach, where consumer, researcher and client work together to arrive at solutions to the problem. This means asking people to do things, not say things: setting a range of 'bite-sized' tasks, telling people what is expected of them and allowing them to take the lead in what they do.

Smaller tasks, which break the problem down into manageable units and give people a range of ways to express themselves, are more likely to access creative thought. There is a wide range of possible activities people might be asked do, such as:

- **Writing exercises:** obituaries, diaries or end of term reports for brands.
- **Construction exercises:** give people a range of materials – paper, card, pictures, string, balloons, magazines – and ask them to build a 'brand room'.
- **Analogical thinking exercises:** considering what a company from a different sector would do under the circumstances, e.g., 'How would Microsoft design a new chocolate bar?' or 'How would Nike advertise a personal pension?'
- **Musical exercises:** giving people a range of music and asking them to select an appropriate soundtrack for a product, brand or idea.
- Exercises to develop an **appropriate language** for the research topic. For example, John Rodgers of The Research Business International often discusses the design of everyday items with respondents prior to introducing any new design ideas. This allows people to develop a language and confidence in discussing design, ensuring that they can engage constructively with the actual subject of the research.

During a project conducted by the author on the re-design of Army recruitment offices, participants were given instamatic cameras during their visits to the office and asked to take pictures of features representing key brand values. The collection of pictures was then used to explore how specific design features evoked certain values. Respondents were also put in teams and asked to spend ten minutes drawing their ideal recruitment office, using large pieces of paper and coloured pens. These methods were particularly useful for those who were less verbally articulate, as they allowed participants to express their creativity through other means. It also allowed them to focus on small, manageable tasks, and then bring together their ideas to build a more complex solution.

Tasks can, of course, be conducted prior to the session and, indeed, for creative workshops or brainstorming sessions this can be very important. Whilst in conventional research the topic is often concealed from respondents because researchers want to get their spontaneous views, in creative projects it is useful to sensitise people to the issue beforehand by getting them to carry out a pre-task. Some pre-tasking can be straightforwardly related to the topic, whilst other tasks can be designed to get people into the style of thinking rather than the specific topic. The following are typical pre-tasks.

- Keeping a diary, either paper or audio, of all occasions when a particular product is used, or when it failed to meet use expectations. For example, researchers might give Dictaphones to respondents and ask them to record any moments when they thought of new uses for their mobile phone, or when their phone lacked a function which they would have found useful (Thomas 2000).
- Interviewing a friend or group of friends about the topic, particularly useful with young people on sensitive topics.
- Taking photographs of things which are important to them and bringing these to the session.
- Looking at a supermarket fixture for a different category, to explore what might be learnt from other areas.
- Avoiding a common product before the session, to heighten awareness of the product category. Gordon (1999a) gives the example of asking participants to avoid drinking tea for a week before a brainstorming session, to make people more aware of the role of tea in their lives.

Bringing the 'Brand Community' Together

Spenser argues that research has traditionally kept the client and the consumer apart, and that this has not helped innovation. However creative the consumers' ideas might be, if they are deliberately kept unaware of the realities of the clients' world their suggestions are unlikely to be directly useful. He suggests that if consumers are informed about the marketing situation and what the client is trying to achieve, they will be in a better position to come up with good ideas. If researchers 'lay their cards on the table', consumers will be more committed and engaged in the process.

If clients and consumers work together directly to solve marketing problems, this has a range of advantages for innovation. The clients, reportedly, become more inspired through direct contact with their consumers, and consumers feel more involved and committed. This means that there is more cross-fertilisation of ideas and that concepts can be developed or discarded much more quickly. Creative personnel and designers can make immediate changes to stimulus materials, without the need for the researcher to return weeks later with the data, only for the client to wonder what would have happened if they had tried a different approach. According to Stephen Wells (Spenser and Wells 2000), a key benefit of this is the energising effect it has on clients, who become more curious about their consumers, more keen to make better products, and more confident to take radical decisions. He gives examples of new brand positionings developed for Olivio, Guinness and Vaseline which he feels were greatly assisted by creative workshops involving consumers and clients.

In addition to bringing client and consumer together, the second way in which the 'brand community' can be united is by bringing together the different people within the client's team. Most frequently researchers will work with either the research manager or the marketing manager, but of course there is a whole range of other functions involved in new pro-duct development: design, packaging, engineering, sales, manufacturing and finance, to name but a few. Running workshops internally within the client organisation, without necessarily involving consumers, can be very productive in helping the client team harness their own resources, and allow a range of different perspectives to be brought to bear in the early stages of development.

Separate Creation from Ordering and Evaluation

A key theme running through all these issues is the need to draw a clear distinction between the three stages of the creative process:

- Creation
- Ordering or theming
- Evaluation.

Stephen Donaldson, Group Insight Manager at Unilever Bestfoods, says that this separation is crucial to effective creativity:

> The benefit is that you then separate building an idea from evaluation. We formally force you to separate these two mindsets and skills. When you do standard focus groups you are relying on the skills of the moderator to interpret consumer reaction, which is essentially both building and evalua-tion wrapped up into one. What we are trying to do is deliberately force the issues apart.

Thus, at the stage of creation and innovation, it is essential to suspend one's rational, evaluative faculties in order not to close down the process of creating too early. If people greet every new idea by wondering 'will it work?' or 'does it make sense?' then they are likely to reject many ideas which, although they might not have been workable themselves, could have prompted others to come up with something better. And more importantly, if people censor their own thinking in this way, they are blocking their own ability to be creative. Thus, at the creative stage it is important to aim for a large number of ideas and to give people licence to come up with ideas which they think are probably unworkable.

The ordering and evaluation of ideas should take place after the creative stage is complete, and should be clearly distinguished from it.

For example, it may take place in a different room, at a different time, or it may actually form part of a different project. When the range of new ideas has been created and people are content that there is nothing to add, *then* the facilitator needs to divide the ideas into grouped themes, see what the broader issues are and evaluate their feasibility according the relevant criteria (marketing, financial, manufacturing, sales, legal, etc.). As Stephen Wells has emphasised, it is important for the facilitator to take the lead on this process to ensure that participants feel there has been a practical outcome and that they have achieved something (Spenser and Wells 2000). Finally, for internal workshops the facilitator needs to gain commitment to action from key individuals, to avoid the syndrome where creative workshops are seen as a day out from the office with no implications for 'real life'.

Examples of Creative Approaches

Many of the approaches described can be integrated into more conventional group discussions, where part of the brief involves innovation and creativity. However, there are also approaches developed specifically for innovation projects.

Brainstorming

Brainstorming is a very common part of idea generation, and usually involves the following steps.

- A theme is identified for the brainstorm. A range of interested participants is invited, usually between 8 and 15.
- A warming-up exercise is conducted at the beginning of the session to break down reservations.
- Criticism and evaluation are forbidden. Participants are encouraged to make statements and not ask questions.
- Freewheeling is encouraged and all ideas, no matter how unconventional, are welcomed.
- Quantity of ideas is sought over quality.
- Building upon the ideas of others is encouraged.

After the brainstorming, the ideas can be grouped by theme and evaluated in a more considered fashion.

Creative Workshops

Creative workshops often involve elements of brainstorming, but can involve larger numbers of people and a wider range of tasks. For example, Pegram Walters conducted workshops for Allied Domecq looking at the lifestyles of young people. They took the radical step of recruiting young people to be their workshop leaders, as they felt this would give them a closer understanding and better relationship with their participants. The process was as follows.

- First, they conducted in-depth interviews to establish broad strategic themes.
- They identified young people from their initial interviews to serve as information-gatherers, i.e., informal researchers who were briefed on the project objectives.
- Then, they recruited 50 young people from the target market to attend evening workshops held in bars. These young people were given various pre-tasks, such as taking photographs to represent their lifestyles, or bringing three things of personal significance.
- During the workshops, the information-gatherers led the participants through a variety of tasks, including the creation of a photomontage using the photos brought by the participants, discussion of specific aspects of their lifestyles, and exercises to explore their relationships with brands.
- These workshops were filmed and recorded. The information-gatherers also attended group debrief sessions the night after the workshops, to get their interpretation of the events.

Sequential Recycling

'Sequential recycling' refers to the process of running group discussions in quick succession on new product or advertising ideas, and making amendments to the ideas after each group. Stephen Donaldson from Unilever Bestfoods describes the process as follows:

> You may stagger groups on Monday, Wednesday, Friday. And then allow yourself to build your ideas and change the stimulus materials. So you are building an idea all the way along ... And then you play around with different things to see if you can unlock what the problem is.

Design or creative personnel should be present during the groups, so they have a clear understanding of consumer reactions and what they can do to improve the idea. Alternatively, the same group can be consulted twice in one day; for example, running a group during the day with the first set of ideas, changing them immediately after the group, and inviting the same people back that evening to see the new work. The advertising agency D'Arcy have used this approach in developing creative work. Business Director David Farrow says that it offers a way of 'trying to get to an idea really fast'. It also allows participants to gain a better understanding of what the creative ideas are trying to achieve, and enhances their involvement and excitement about the process.

Thus, qualitative researchers already possess many of the skills required to facilitate innovation and creativity. They can put people at ease, encourage them to interact and use a range of techniques to help people see things in new ways. However, they need to shift their mindset away from the priorities of the researcher – reliability, robustness of data, understanding and explanation through verbal reasoning – towards the priorities of creativity – a task-focused, freewheeling approach, bringing together different perspectives, concerned with outcomes rather than processes. Indeed, it is uncertain whether the activity researchers would thus be engaging in should be called research at all, a point to which I shall return at the end of this chapter.

RESEARCHING THE FUTURE

The role of research in exploring the future, as discussed above, is a vexed issue. It appears to be generally accepted that the postmodern condition makes it very difficult for researchers to predict future trends. The pace of change, the speed of technological development, and the extent of global interconnections via the media make it impossible to predict with certainty whether a particular advertising strategy or brand will succeed in the long term. And there are also deeper philosophical problems with the idea that the past can ever form a reliable guide to the future. However, researchers writing on this issue often appear ambivalent. They accept the theoretical point that firm predictions are not possible, but they nevertheless frequently reintroduce the idea through some other means. Thus, Fuller and Collier (1999: 1) state that 'many aspects of the future brand and advertising landscape *are* unpredictable' (emphasis in original), but then describe their own methods as 'predictive or forward looking research'. Gordon (1999a: 293) tells us that research is rarely accurate at predicting what people will do in the future, but later suggests that 'good researchers … are able to spot trends at least a year before they are noticed by the media or brand owners', which she attributes to 'intuition'.

So, what are we to make of these apparent contradictions? It seems that researchers have accepted at the level of theory that they cannot predict the future with certainty, but in practice researchers feel that their experience and intuition, combined with research skills, allow them to make a pretty good guess. Indeed, in the author's opinion, this is a much more realistic description of the role of researchers in predicting the future – we know that our predictions are partial and uncertain, but we can nevertheless make a good guess. Contrary to Mark Earls' advice (2001), I believe researchers can help companies dealing with the future in at least two important ways:

- By using their experience, knowledge of the consumer, research skills and intuition to make educated guesses about future trends.
- By assisting organisations in developing and planning for a range of future options which may or may not come to pass.

Trend-Spotting

Trend-spotting is one of the most popular new areas for marketing and research consultancies (Gordon 1999a; Pillot De Chenecey 2000). Trend-spotting is not concerned with providing certainty regarding what will happen in the future, but rather with exploring the cultural trends that may influence companies, brands or social policies. Trend-spotters look for emergent opportunities, product areas that seem to be opening up, new ideas about brand relationships which may exist only among a very small section of the current population, but seem to constitute the direction in which things are moving.

Trend-spotting can be done without actually conducting consumer research, by using aspects of popular culture as data, as discussed in Chapter 5 on Cultural Analysis. More commonly, however, it relies on the idea that some consumers – leading edge, early adopters, whatever – are ahead of the rest of the market. What these consumers are doing today, the mainstream will do tomorrow. Fuller and Collier (1999: 1) state that a 'leading edge consumer … in some way represents the consumer of the future'. By researching the attitudes, aspirations and values of these 'leading edge consumers', one can gain an insight into the future of the mainstream market. Thus, as Holder and Young (1997) point out, 'the future is with us – now'.

The key issue in this form of trend-spotting is to identify the most relevant group of leading edge consumers, and Fuller and Collier emphasise that someone who may be leading edge in one category could be entirely mainstream in another. For example, a consumer who is at the forefront of technological change may have a thoroughly mainstream taste in music. Or a leading edge consumer in the fashion market may be very conventional in their working practices. They also suggest that the most relevant groups to include may not even be consumers of the product being researched. For example, when Flamingo were looking at new design ideas for an alcoholic drink, they recruited people such as photographers, designers and television producers to discuss the concepts. These people were not the target audience for the product, but were recruited 'because they have an acute sensitivity to the direction of change in the language of design' (Fuller and Collier 1999: 6). Their reactions to the design ideas could therefore be seen as indicative of what the mass market might think in six months' time. Similarly, when looking at trends in the male fashion market, they focused on gay men, on the grounds that gay men have frequently been at the forefront of developments in male fashion which have later 'trickled down' to the mainstream. And they report that when Microsoft want to find out about how relationships with technology are changing, they recruit people according to the type of company they work in and their style of work, rather than their job function. This is based on the assumption that some working practices (e.g., working from home, self-employment, portfolio careers) indicate the direction of the future, and these people will therefore be able to provide an insight into how the mainstream will be using technology in the future.

Flamingo's work concerns brand development, whereas a slightly different approach has been developed by Holder and Young (1997) for looking at products and services. Holder and Young also base their work on the assumption that some consumers are 'ahead of the game'. Because of their particular interest in the product or service area, they are more likely to be aware of trends in the market and to see new product opportunities. Thus, Holder and Young advise recruiting respondents who are 'highly involved in a particular subject area yet currently achieving low satisfaction'. Their approach then relies on working with these consumers on a long-term basis, involving clients directly in the process, to find better solutions to product and service problems. The research allows the participants to set their own agenda and pursue this in collaboration with researchers and clients, and Holder and Young argue that the passion and commitment brought by these more involved consumers contrasts sharply with the unhelpfulness of talking to consumers who are 'bored, complacent or content'. Among the main advantages of their approach, they suggest, are the speed with which new ideas can be generated, a reduction in product failure and an enhancement of the insight the client has about the consumer of the future.

Another method related to trend-spotting is the **Delphi technique**, named after the Greek oracle. This is based on the assumption that the collective view of a group of experts is likely to give a good indication of the future in a particular field. The technique tries to aim for a consensus between the experts by sharing their views in a structured fashion over a period of time. A panel of relevant experts is recruited and sent (most commonly by e-mail) a set of questions on which their views are sought. In quantitative exercises the questions may be quite precise, asking by what date they believe a particular event may occur. But in qualitative exercises the questions are more likely to be general, asking about perceptions of future developments in a particular area. The responses are then collated and summarised, and e-mailed again to the group for further comments. This process is continued until a consensus is reached, or until the researcher feels they have gained enough data.

The Delphi technique is different because the experts are asked their *opinion* on the future – they are not assumed to represent the future in some way. Trend-spotting and 'future featuring' rely upon the idea that some consumers are already living the future – 'leading edge consumers' – or they have particular insights into where the future might lie – 'future featurers'. For all three methods, recruitment of the right participants is essential, and, as Fuller and Collier point out, this requires a more active and analytical approach to research design.

Thus, Fuller and Collier, and Holder and Young, argue that research can provide a good idea of where the future may lie. Although they do not explicitly state this, it is clear that their work relies not just upon research skills, but also on their experience of the market and their knowledge of where the relevant influences are likely to come from. This means that there must always be a degree of uncertainty in their educated guesses, and in the author's opinion it would strengthen the position of research if we made this clear to our clients. Even if we cannot give the firm predictions which our clients may hope for, we can indicate the trends that influence their brands, products and services; we can identify emergent opportunities and unspoken needs; and we can suggest ways in which they can shape the future in line with their business strategies. These are important achievements, and they show that the absence of certainty by no means implies the impossibility of educated guesses.

Scenario Planning

However, the more researchers broaden their vision to the longer term and the bigger picture, the less effectively they can predict the direction of change in markets and social issues. While research may be able to provide a reasonable idea, through the methods outlined above, of emerging opportunities in the mobile phone market over the next year, it is much less able to predict the demand for private health care over the next ten years, or the size of the market for cars in 20 years' time. This is because the range of factors that influence these issues is too great, and the timescales are too long, to confidently forecast what the future may hold.

In these contexts, scenario planning may be a useful approach. The technique was pioneered by oil companies in the 1970s after many failed to predict the rise in oil prices, assuming that demand and supply would remain stable (Ringland 1998: 16–23). The difficulties they had in adapting to the changed situation prompted them to consider planning for a range of longer-term options. Scenario planning explicitly recognises the unpredictability of the future, but also accepts that decisions need to be taken which will impact on the future. It does not produce forecasts, but rather develops alternative scenarios about what might happen. Scenario planning may be used to:

- Develop a range of different scenarios for the future, which can be used to plan strategy and decision-making.
- Develop a single vision of what a corporation or organisation wants to achieve in the future, and then decide what the organisation can do to make its desired future more likely, and to pre-empt the less desirable outcomes.

A typical scenario planning event might involve the following stages.

- Identify the topic and the time frame for the scenarios – usually a time frame of ten years or more would be appropriate.

- Gather together the key stakeholders who will have to use the scenarios.
- Identify the driving forces which impact on the scenarios, and the trends within these drivers.
- Create and name the scenario, which should be contrasting and provocative, but plausible rather than 'off the wall'.
- Apply the scenarios to key decisions or areas, e.g., 'If Scenario A were to occur, what implications would this have for our product development plans?'

For example, the Local Government Association produced a scenario planning exercise for local authorities to assess how well adapted they would be to three different futures:

1 **Modernised Markets**, which assumes high but variable economic growth, a prosperous but divided society, and a government that emphasises competition and individual freedom.
2 **A New Dimension**, which assumes fairly high but stable economic growth, a cohesive society, and a governmental emphasis on social cohesion and civil society.
3 **On the Edge**, where economic growth is low, society is poor and divided, and government is centralised and authoritarian.

These scenarios are designed to help councils think through how they might react to these futures, and of course also to consider how they could prevent the less desirable options from becoming realities.

Community visions are a variant of scenario planning used in the public sector to develop a shared vision of the future for a particular area. The technique is most useful for defined geographical areas, and therefore can be used by local councils to involve residents in creating an idea of the future which people can agree with and work towards. It is important for community visions that a range of local residents and other key stake-holders is involved in the process, so that the vision developed can be owned by the widest range of local people. And importantly, unlike in many other research exercises, the participants are trying to arrive at a consensus on the future for their area.

A community visioning exercise would be similar to scenario planning as outlined above, with the exception that the participants would try to agree on the *ideal* future for their area, the possible barriers to achieving this, and what actions need to be taken by the key stakeholders in order to make the vision a reality. For example, the London Borough of Lewisham held a one-day Vision for Older People event. This involved inviting about 80 'old people of the future', i.e., 40–60-year-olds, to a conference. Facts and figures about Lewisham were presented and people were divided into smaller groups with facilitators to discuss their hopes and aspirations for old age, and the results were used by the council in developing their strategy for older people. In this context, qualitative methods can help identify and shape a desired future, rather than merely try to predict it.

CONCLUSIONS

Businesses have become increasingly concerned with innovation and creativity over the past decade. The need to produce new products, advertising or branding ideas to attract the attention of over supplied, cynical consumers is at the heart of many corporations. Change is now seen as a constant feature of business life, rather than a one-off event followed by a period of stability. And in this fast-moving business context, the future is seen as unpredictable, with yesterday only a partial guide to tomorrow.

This has created problems for research, which has been accused of failing to meet the challenges and priorities of 'The Creative Age', where being first to come up with a new idea is what counts. Research has been criticised as focusing on the past, using outdated models of linear thinking, failing to see the big picture and the emerging opportunities, stifling creativity and being of little help in facilitating innovation. And qualitative research in particular has suffered from these accusations, associated with the iconic image of the 'focus group' killing off delicate creative ideas. In response to these criticisms, qualitative researchers have developed various new methods designed specifically to help with creative processes and idea generation. There has been a move to separate processes of creation from evaluation, and to work with consumers who indicate where the future might lie, rather than merely replaying the past. And qualitative research has developed and borrowed planning methods that recognise the uncertainty of the future, but nevertheless attempt to assist in understanding and shaping it.

However, although qualitative researchers frequently conduct creative workshops, brainstorming sessions, sequential recycling and community visioning, it is by no means certain that these new methods should be termed 'research'. Although similar skills are used, they are evaluated according to quite different criteria. Indeed, research-based criteria might be actively detrimental to the facilitation of creativity – can one imagine a 'reliable creative idea', or a 'representative innovation'? Researchers involved in facilitating innovation need to be very clear that their clients are not getting fast and dirty research. Rather, skilled researchers are using their qualitative skills to help facilitate processes of innovation and creativity. If researchers ensure that they, and their clients, are clear about this, they can free themselves to deploy their skills in a much wider arena; if they do not, they run the risk of misleading their clients and blurring their own understanding of what constitutes qualitative research.

KEY POINTS

- A range of changes in the marketing context have made it more difficult for researchers to forecast the future based on past trends. These include:

  o the fast pace of technological development;
  o the rate of change in some markets, especially youth sectors;
  o the range of influences on consumers and markets, which may be local, regional, or global.

- Qualitative research has also been criticised for stifling creativity. Although some of these criticisms are unfounded, there is a real conflict between the research mindset – focusing on rigour, reliability and analytical logic – and the creative mindset – concerned with play, unexpected connections and intuitive insight.
- In order to be more open to creative processes, qualitative researchers have made several changes to their standard practices. They have:

  o moved away from 'normative consumers', focusing instead on anyone who can tell us something useful;
  o shifted from a question and answer format to a task-based format, focusing on outcomes rather than processes;
  o brought together divergent points of view rather than keeping them apart;
  o separated the process of creation from evaluation in the research design.

- Although researchers cannot predict the future with certainty, they can make educated guesses about emergent trends and future possibilities. Working with 'leading edge' consumers, or those with a strong interest in the product, can assist in identifying trends, but researchers must acknowledge that their guesses rely on judgement and intuition as well as research data.
- In the longer term, researchers can help clients develop strategies for alternative future possibilities, using scenario planning techniques. These methods can also help clients identify actions that need to be taken to achieve their future goals.
- Brainstorming, trend-spotting and scenario planning allow the use of qualitative skills in a wider arena, but they are not primarily research techniques and are judged by different criteria.

Research and Consultation
in the Public Sector

This chapter describes the use of qualitative research in the public sector, specifically in the field know as 'consultation'. First the drivers of research in the public sector are described, outlining the changes in public expectations and legislative frameworks which have prompted local authorities, health authorities and other bodies to conduct research. Discussion follows of the key differences between public and private sector research, pointing out in particular that the notion of 'consultation' requires *both* the generation of useful data, and *also* the development of a positive relationship between the public and the service provider. This dual focus means that conventional qualitative research methods need to be adapted if they are used as part of consultation processes, and also that alternative methods may sometimes need to be developed. The chapter concludes by discussing the specific new methods developed for consultation in the public sector, and suggests that their commercial sector potential remains undeveloped.

THE PUBLIC SECTOR: AN EXPANDING AREA FOR RESEARCH AND CONSULTATION

Thus far, this book has concentrated mainly on research methods developed and used within the private sector. We have focused on issues such as advertising, branding and new product development, and explored how alternative methods can assist in these processes. This chapter focuses on approaches that have been developed in the public sector in the UK, although it also draws upon methods first used in the USA and in Germany. As pointed out in a recent Cabinet Office guide (Cabinet Office 1998), in the private sector the reasons for conducting research are clear – companies need to meet their customers' needs or people will go elsewhere. However, in the public sector this is usually not the case – we cannot decide which local authority will collect the rubbish from our homes, who we want to pay our taxes to, or which police force we will call in an emergency. Although there is increasing choice in the public sector, competition between service providers is not a major driver of research. Nevertheless, over the past decade public sector organisations have considerably expanded the amount of research they carry out. Political parties, central government departments, local authorities, health authorities, and police forces, among others, have all been 'consulting the public' via qualitative and quantitative methods, and all the signs are that this trend is set to grow (Hedges and Duncan 2000; Local Government Association 2000; Mattinson and Bell 2000).

However, in spite of this growth of research in the public sector, some commissioning organisations have found that traditional qualitative and quantitative methods do not fully meet their requirements. Although clearly valuable for accessing the views of the public, they are less well adapted to engaging and involving people in decision-making processes. These latter points, whilst rarely important in the commercial sector, are often important additional goals in public sector projects. So, why has this field grown so rapidly over the past decade, and what are the differences which the commercial researcher should bear in mind when working in this new and unfamiliar environment? These are the questions addressed in this chapter. From the perspective of the commercial researcher, the chapter aims to fulfil three objectives:

- To outline the differences between research in the private and public sectors. This provides an understanding of the priorities and context of government-funded research and, hopefully, will help researchers avoid the misunderstandings that can arise from the differing expectations of the private and public sectors.
- To describe some of the new methods which have developed in the public sector to address these different needs, methods that commercial researchers can employ with public sector clients.
- To suggest how these methods might apply in the commercial sector, where as yet there is limited evidence of their use.

The Drivers of Research

The expansion of public sector research can be traced to a range of factors coming together over the past decade, including the influence of private sector thinking and also legislative requirements to consult with the public (Hedges and Duncan 2000; Local Government Association 2000; Martin 1998). Some of the key factors include:

- The influence of the 'customer service revolution' in the 1980s in finance and retailing, where service quality was seen as key to commercial success. This led to raised expectations of service from public sector bodies, and to the introduction of various 'Citizens' Charters' under the Conservative administration, specifying the levels of service provided by schools, doctors' surgeries and various central government departments. In this way, the idea of a customer focus was introduced into the public sector, which had previously been very supplier-focused.

- The realisation from the experiences of the 1980s that top-down approaches to urban regeneration and community development rarely work, and that social programmes are most effective when local people are involved in their development and delivery. This has resulted in central government funding for many important regeneration programmes, such as the City Challenge or the Single Regeneration Budget, being dependent on consultation with local people.
- The rise of 'evidence-based policy', suggesting that policy initiatives should be derived from firm evidence of 'what works', rather than unsubstantiated or ideological views about what should work.
- New legislative requirements have been placed upon local authorities, health authorities and police forces to consult with local people. The Crime and Disorder Act 1998 obliges local authorities and police forces to consult with the public prior to formulating their Community Safety Plans. Health authorities are obliged to consult on major changes to service provision. And the Local Government Act 1999 introduced the concept of 'Best Value' for local authorities, which obliges them to consult with service users and tax payers to determine levels of satisfaction with service provision.
- There has been a growing concern about the gap between the public and the democratic processes, often termed the 'democratic deficit' (Coote and Mattinson 1997). Voter turnout in elections is falling, with around 60 per cent voting in the 2001 UK General Election, whilst for local government elections participation can be as low as 20 per cent. Many people believe that mainstream politics is irrelevant to their lives, and they feel little sense of engagement with local decision-making (Desai and Thomas 1998; Lovell and Henderson 2000). This reduces the legitimacy of local political representation, and undermines the role of local government – if so few people care about local government, what gives local authorities the right to demand taxes and claim to represent the public? Thus, various methods to re-engage people in political processes and local decision-making have developed. These methods often appear similar to commercial qualitative research methods, but they have an additional purpose – citizen involvement, as well as data collection.

The London Borough of Lewisham has been at the forefront of these developments, and various examples will be drawn from their work throughout this chapter. Guy Rubin, Principal Policy Officer (Democracy and Consultation) in the Policy and Partnership Unit, explains how Lewisham's consultation strategy developed:

> It stems from an analysis from Members and Officers some years ago around what was termed the Democratic Deficit. This is the idea that the community was becoming more and more alienated or was drifting apart from the Council and you get this perception that the Council did lots of

things and nobody knew because they weren't consulted. Councillors and Officers at Lewisham set up this project called the Democracy Project and the idea was to explicitly try and address this. And to experiment with a whole range of different methods to see whether we could have an impact on this and to try and reach a stage where the community was being consulted on key policy decisions and the results were being fed back to them. Instead of people saying, well we only see our Councillors every 4 or 5 years, to try and build up a more organic process in which there was feedback in the community both ways.

Thus, the main agenda for local authorities is one of public consultation and involvement – finding ways to engage people in the democratic process. Research often forms part of this process, but in consultation projects the collection of data is rarely the sole objective.

Research and Consultation

As pointed out by Hedges and Duncan (2000), there are many public sector research projects in which data collection is the main objective – evaluating the effectiveness of new policies, or exploring how best to implement them. In these projects, there is no assumption that the public will be involved in the final decision-making process, nor that the results will be fed back to participants. However, in other public sector projects, particularly those carried out by local authorities in the field of consultation, these expectations are relevant. It is therefore important for researchers to know what their clients' expectations are, and to distinguish clearly between research and consultation processes.

Research and consultation are often confused, both by researchers and commissioning organisations. For example, a recent brief received by the author from a national public sector organisation was headed 'Research Brief', but two pages later stated that 'the consultation must involve the widest possible range of organisations'. Without an understanding of the democratic role of consultations, it is hard for a researcher to see the point of such statements. Indeed, most government guides produced for public sector bodies (Cabinet Office 1998; Martin 1998) refer to 'consulting users' or 'involving users' – they are not guides to research. Rather, they discuss the use of research methods as *part* of consultation programmes, and it is important to make clear that consultation involves more than just research. Indeed, it is common to distinguish between the following models in the public sector:

- **Research model:** finding out people's attitudes and views, but keeping control of the decision-making firmly within the commissioning body.
- **Consultation model:** finding out attitudes and views, asking people what their preferences and priorities are, but offering limited scope to influence the decisions.

- **Participation model:** involving the public in decision-making through dialogue and negotiation, but keeping the final say within the commissioning body.
- **Delegation model:** giving local people direct control over budgets and strategies, and allowing them to make their own decisions.
  (From Hedges and Duncan 2000: 199)

In practice, elements of these different models may overlap, but it does constitute a useful way to clarify the differences between research and consultation. Research should form part of consultation or public partici-pation programmes. The views of a representative range of the popula-tion should be gained, using reliable methods, in order to avoid domination of the agenda by vocal minorities. And those methods may need to be adapted to ensure that useful data is gained on the often complex issues addressed.

However, research does not *constitute* consultation, and a failure to distinguish between the two lies at the heart of many of the misunder-standings that arise between commercial research agencies and public sector commissioning bodies. Public sector clients often assume when they commission a commercial agency to conduct research that they have commissioned a consultation programme. Research agencies, on the other hand, see their key task as gathering data in a structured fashion, and view the client's expectations of public involvement as bizarre and irrelevant to the research process.

The purpose of this chapter is to clarify the issues that commercial researchers need to bear in mind when working in this growing but often unfamiliar field.

WHAT IS DIFFERENT ABOUT THE PUBLIC SECTOR?

Qualitative methods are increasingly popular among public sector organi-sations. They are seen as more involving, more engaging and more fun than drier quantitative approaches, and therefore can be seen as intrinsically better adapted to getting the public actively involved in local decision-making (Fawcett and Laird 2001). However, without an understanding of the different requirements of public sector bodies, researchers may find it hard to meet their clients' needs, or even understand their priorities. This section discusses those needs and priorities, divided into three categories:

1 **Target audiences:** the target audiences for public sector research are often wider than for commercial studies, and can be alienated and cynical about the commissioning bodies.
2 **Complex topics:** the issues addressed in the public sector can be more complex than those in commercial research, meaning that people need to be given information and time to digest it before coming to a view.

3   **Trade-offs and conflicts:** public sector organisations often need to balance competing interests and arrive at a conclusion which is acceptable to everyone.

In consultation processes, there is an assumption that participants should be told the outcomes of the process, and have some way to influence the decisions taken as a result. Thus, this section concludes with some discusion of **feedback and involvement**.

Target Audiences

Commercial companies can decide on their target audience and aim their advertising and products at this group. They can focus on the most profitable sectors and decide that they do not want to provide a service to the rest of the population – some banks and airlines quite explicitly take this approach. Public sector service providers, on the other hand, have a duty to make their services accessible to everyone. They need to think about the fairness of their activities, and they need to make sure that minorities are catered for as well as the majority. Groups often under-represented in commercial research – ethnic minorities, homeless people, drug users, ex-offenders, the long-term unemployed – need to be specifically targeted when working in the public sector.

Also, many people feel little connection to or engagement with public sector bodies. They may believe that their views will not be taken seriously or make any difference to local services, and that it is not worth getting involved in research or consultation exercises (Desai and Thomas 1998; Lovell and Henderson 2000). For these groups, researchers may need to convince people that it is worth taking part. This is often a question of allowing people a real role in setting the agenda for the project, so that the things that are genuinely important to them can be addressed. For example, when setting up qualitative panels or forums (discussed below), it can be helpful for the panel members themselves to decide what they want to focus on rather than being given a topic by the commissioning body. This can provide a greater sense of involvement and empowerment among those taking part, and clearly has similarities to the future featuring approach discussed in the previous chapter.

Innovative approaches can also help catch the attention of those traditionally not interested in local politics. For example, Lewisham Council ran a project called Your Choice Your Vote – the Lewisham Young People's Referendum – in order to encourage young people to get involved with the local council. First, a series of workshops were held among local young people to identify the issues that were most important to them. From these workshops, three projects were identified which were likely to interest young people – a local youth newspaper, a project focusing on teenage pregnancy, or a CD ROM on the topic of racism. Young people were asked to vote – via their schools and colleges – on the project they wanted to take forward, and the CD ROM was the winner. The results were fed back to each young person by a personal letter, which also invited them to take part in the production of the CD ROM. The purpose of this exercise was not primarily to get the young people's views, but also to convince them via this innovative approach and tangible outcome that it was worthwhile getting involved in local council activities.

Complex Topics

Another problem in public sector research is that people frequently know very little about the topics being discussed. Although they might have experience of using the services, they often do not know which services are provided by which local bodies. For example, in research for local authorities people frequently want to discuss hospitals and policing. However, these are not provided by the local authority, and the council's influence on them is limited. Also, local authorities are obliged to consult with the public on a new range of options for the structure of local government. Local authorities are moving away from old committee-based systems, and can choose between three different options for new styles of local government – a cabinet and directly elected mayor, a cabinet and a council leader elected by the cabinet, and a cabinet and council manager who is appointed rather than elected. However, most people do not know what the current structure is, so it can be difficult to express a view on the benefits of possible changes. As Robin Clarke, head of the Public Involvement Programme at the Institute for Public Policy Research (IPPR), points out, 'local authorities want something that is useful, that can add to policy. You don't want something that just says, "well, the public don't know anything about that".'

The issues on which views are sought are often complex and require people to consider a range of different factors before coming to a view. Whilst there is always some benefit in knowing what people's 'knee jerk' response to an issue might be, this initial response is often of limited use to public policy-makers. For example, the fact that people are worried about 'Frankenstein Foods' (genetically modified foods) but do not understand the science involved is worth knowing, but it does not help formulate a balanced and acceptable policy on genetic modification. Health authorities frequently consult on emotive issues such as the prioritisation of health care – should funding prioritise expensive treatment for a few, such as heart bypass operations, or less expensive treatment for many, such as hip replacements? Also common are consultations on re-organisation of hospital services, often involving the closure of small local hospitals and the centralisation of expertise in larger specialist units. And the Wellcome Trust recently conducted research on public attitudes to human cloning, which required respondents to understand a range of scientific concepts.

For these sorts of issues, researchers need to give people:

(a) clear, balanced information which is easy to understand; and
(b) time and space to consider the issues before having to express their opinion.

It is preferable for people to have the chance to discuss the issue away from the research context – in their family, workplace and social circle. Frequently, a single group discussion is not enough to do justice to these sorts of issues. For the research on human cloning, the Wellcome Trust (1998) commissioned reconvened group discussions. The first groups concentrated on getting people's uninformed opinions, and at the end of this group they were given information about human genetics to take away. The second sessions focused on the more informed views, and on the extent to which people had changed their minds on the issue as a result of receiving information. On a smaller scale, when Lewisham Council wanted to consult the public on its budget plan, they convened group discussions which were attended by a researcher and council officer. The council officer made a short presentation about the budget, answered questions and then withdrew so the researcher could explore people's attitudes. And on a larger scale, Citizens' Juries and deliberative polls give people several days to consider the topic under discussion.

Trade-offs and Conflicts

Hedges and Duncan (2000) point out that research in the public sector is often concerned with trade-offs, and with balancing different, sometimes conflicting demands. People's attitudes are frequently self-contradictory, but few of us are forced to arrive at rational and consistent views on key public issues. We can tell opinion pollsters that we want better public services and lower taxation; that we want lower pollution and unrestricted car use; animal welfare and cheap food. However, public policy-makers need to trade off between these options, and ideally they need to know what form of trade-off the public would prefer. This means using more deliberative methods, such as Citizens' Juries or deliberative polls (discussed below) which give people the chance to weigh up the evidence, consider the options, discuss them with others and then express their views.

Public policy-makers also need to reconcile the conflicting demands of different groups, and to arrive at solutions that are acceptable, if not actually welcomed, by the majority of the population. For example, residents frequently object to sites for travellers being placed near their homes, but local authorities have a duty to house travellers and therefore have to place the site somewhere. Older residents on a housing estate may want to stop young people playing football outside their flats, but the young people may have nowhere else to play. People with mental health problems may prefer to live in the community rather than be isolated, but mothers of young children may find their behaviour disturbing even if they present no threat in reality. In these sorts of situations, people need to look beyond their own immediate concerns and consider the wider good of the whole community. Conducting separate group discussions among the interested parties on any of these examples would probably only reinforce their different opinions. Bringing together the different groups to deliberate, consider each other's perspectives and arrive at a consensus may be a more productive way to arrive at a useful outcome.

Feedback and Involvement

The three issues discussed above – inclusive target audiences, the complexity of the issues and the need to reconcile conflicting points of view – are all relevant to the 'research model' as well as to the 'consultation' or 'participation' models discussed above. However, if research is conducted as part of a consultation exercise, there is also an expectation that participants will receive feedback from the process and have some form of involvement in the decision-making process.

Indeed, a common complaint from people involved in public sector consultations is that they do not receive feedback after taking part. This fuels the circle of alienation, with people being less likely to take part in future (Desai and Thomas 1998). Thus, letting people know the results of consultations should be seen as integral to the process rather than an optional add-on. People need to know what was said and, more importantly, what action the authority is going to take. Lewisham Council's Citizens' Panel provides respondents with a newsletter outlining results of each wave of interviewing, and what action the council will be taking as a result. Other local authorities frequently report the results of consultations and surveys in their local papers.

Ideally, consultations should be tied to specific decisions which the authority needs to make, and there should be transparent and credible mechanisms to see how the decision has been influenced. There is little point carrying out a consultation if the commissioning organisation does not intend to act upon the results. For example, in Citizens' Juries it is common for the 'jurors' to present their recommendations directly to the commissioning authority, which is then expected to make a formal response. This enhances the authority and the credibility of the consultation, and ensures that the results of the consultation cannot be 'swept under the carpet'.

As pointed out above, consultation exercises are not just about gathering data – they also aim to build the capacity of local communities to get involved in decision-making. Those who take part in consultations, particularly the more deliberative methods, should feel that they have learnt something, they have influenced local decision-making, their views are valued and that it is worthwhile getting involved in local democratic processes. Some participants in consultation projects get involved in longer-term planning with the local authority, especially when the commissioning organisation realises that the consultees may have acquired specialist knowledge which could help them in designing and delivering local services. George Street Research (Fawcett and Laird 2001) interviewed those who had taken part in consultations and those who had commissioned them on behalf of the Scottish Executive. They found that there was little 'hard' evidence of the 'larger goals of social capital building and community empowerment' being achieved. However, participants did become more knowledgeable and confident at holding policy-makers to account (2001: 307–8), and the commissioners believed there had been positive benefits in building relationships with the communities.

In some cases, however, the consultation may identify the need for more support to help local people get involved in policy-making. For example, in order to participate fully in consultation exercises people need time, commitment, access to information, an understanding of the political process and the confidence to make their views heard and hold policy-makers to account. Thus, some consultation approaches include an element of training and support for local people and community groups in order to help them get involved. This might include training local residents to carry out interviews on their estate, or funding a local youth group to set up a monthly meeting among young people in a locality.

For example, in research conducted by the author for one London borough, it was found that there were very few active Asian community organisations in the local area. The Asian population was quite small and dispersed, and this made it hard for the council – and indeed the researchers – to access the views of this section of the population. One of the research recommendations was therefore that the council should support local community organisations, providing them with some training or resources to help them engage in council consultation procedures. These activities would not normally be seen as part of a research project, but they may form an integral part of a consultation process.

Thus, qualitative research is frequently used in the public sector, but there are some important differences that commercial researchers need to bear in mind if they are working in this field. If researchers are to meet their clients' expectations they may need to reach out to marginalised social groups, explain complex issues in a simple fashion, work towards consensus on controversial issues, and provide feedback to participants if conducting a consultation exercise. In many cases, these requirements may be met through adapting conventional qualitative method, such as using reconvened groups, longer workshops, or more creative stimulus materials. However, there is also a range of alternative methods which have been developed to meet the specific needs of the public sector, and these are discussed below.

SPECIFIC QUALITATIVE APPROACHES

Deliberative Methods

The issues addressed in public sector research are often complex and require time to for a considered opinion to be reached. In the private sector this is not so important; we do not usually need to tell consumers the relative cost and reach of different media when researching advertising, or the increase in sales that would be required to maintain profit margins while reducing prices when researching promotions. In the public sector, however, it is important that people understand the full picture, because research commissioners want their decisions to be seen as legitimate by the public. Thus, if one is conducting a project about prioritising health care – hip replacements versus heart surgery, for example – it is important to tell people the relative costs and effectiveness of these procedures, and allow them time to come to a view. This has resulted in the development of various deliberative methods, all of which have the following features in common:

- They allow people time to consider the issues, sometimes several days.
- They provide information and allow people to question professionals.
- They put diverse groups of people together, ensuring that participants hear points of view which contrast to their own.
- They aim for some sort of consensual outcome which people can agree on as a course of action (with the exception of deliberative polls).

The key idea underlying deliberative methods is that when ordinary people are presented with clear, unbiased information about complex issues, they can understand the topics and make sensible recommendations. However, in everyday life we do not have access to such information, nor time to consider the issues. Thus, in quantitative surveys and, to a lesser extent, conventional qualitative research, people give uninformed opinions on complex issues which, in many cases, they have never thought about before. In contrast, the results of Citizens' Juries and deliberative polls are assumed – within certain limits – to represent what the public *would* think *if* they were informed and engaged citizens. They are therefore thought to provide a truer representation of informed public opinion.

Citizens' Juries are probably the best known deliberative method. The technique was developed in the United States and Germany to involve ordinary people in complex decisions and to challenge politicians (Coote and Mattinson 1997). In the UK, it has been used by health authorities and local authorities, and has been pioneered by a few key organisations. Opinion Leader Research – a London-based research consultancy – and the Institute for Public Policy Research – a UK independent 'think-tank' – have conducted a series of pilot juries in collaboration with health authorities, and the Local Government Management Board have conducted pilot juries in collaboration with local authorities. Since then, they have grown in popularity and been used by many local councils and health authorities (Institute for Public Policy Research, 2000), frequently to address high profile decisions where there is genuine uncertainty about the best way to proceed.

Coote and Mattinson (1997) outline the key characteristics of a Citizens' Jury as follows:

- Between 12 and 16 ordinary members of the public are recruited to represent a cross-section of the local population.
- They are asked to consider a significant local or national issue and are given a briefing session.
- The jury sits for four days, with moderators to facilitate the discussion.
- They are fully informed about the question being considered, and they receive evidence from a selection of 'witnesses', including experts in the field and lay people affected by the issue.
- They question the witnesses, discuss the issue in small groups and plenary sessions, and can request more information or ask to speak to the witnesses again.
- On the final day, they draw their conclusions, which are compiled in a report.
- They submit their report to the commissioning authority, which is expected to make a formal response.

The advantages of a Citizens' Jury are the depth of consideration people can give to the issue, the fact that complex topics can be addressed and that the jury's report usually makes more impact than a standard research report. Also, they frequently attract media attention, and therefore are a good way for an authority to demonstrate publicly its commitment to taking local people's views seriously.

However, there are also weaknesses to the process. The small sample must call into question the representativeness of the jurors' recommendations, even if they do form a cross-section of the population. They are also highly dependent on the quality of information provided and the range of witnesses, and the process could be biased by partial information. It can be difficult to explain the jurors' recommendations to the rest of the public who have not been through the deliberative procedure, and jurors can also make recommendations which are beyond the remit of the commissioning body, or which would require legal changes. Finally, of course, the process requires great commitment from the commissioning body and is very expensive – typically around £20,000 at the time of writing.

The Citizens' Jury conducted by Lewisham Council and Opinion Leader Research provides a good example of these issues in practice. In 1996 Lewisham Council held a Citizens' Jury on the question 'What can be done to reduce harm to the community and individuals from drugs?' This issue was chosen because it was a high profile issue and one on which the council felt that the media and other sources of information had misinformed the public. Thus, it was a topic which would interest people and would benefit from a more considered approach. The jury followed the format described above and, according to Stella Clarke (Clarke 1998), the process confirmed that ordinary people can engage in complex issues, listen to others, change their opinions as a result of hearing evidence, and make useful policy recommendations. However, the jury also made recommendations which fell outside the remit of the council, such as considering the legalisation of cannabis, and a wider use of prescribed diamorphine (clinical heroin) for addicts. These issues would be the responsibility of the Home Office, and therefore the council could only lobby central government rather than take action itself.

Deliberative polls are similar to Citizens' Juries, but they attempt to quantify the outcome of the deliberative process. The method was developed in the United States by Professor James Fishkin, a political scientist, to discover what an informed public would think about key issues of public concern. The process is similar to the Citizens' Jury described above, with the following differences.

- Prior to the deliberative process, a random sample survey of the population is conducted on the issue under consideration. This is to determine their views before they are given any information, to allow the researchers to measure attitudinal changes.
- A representative sub-sample is recruited from the main sample, and this sample is large enough for quantitative analysis – between 250 and 300.
- This sub-sample is invited to what is, in effect, a very large Citizens' Jury as described above.
- After the event, participants complete an identical questionnaire to the one filled in initially, in order to assess how their attitudes have changed.

The deliberative poll therefore aims to provide the 'best of both worlds' – representative quantitative sampling and a high level of deliberation. In the UK, such polls have been conducted by the National Centre for Social Research in collaboration with the television company Channel Four, and have been televised media events. They have usually addressed large-scale national issues such as the economy, the National Health Service, crime and the European Union. The results have justified Professor Fishkin's view that people would change their views if exposed to informed debate. For example, the sample moved towards a more liberal position on criminal justice, and in one case substantially changed voting intentions (Park 1998). Its most obvious disadvantage is the huge expense involved, with one government guide estimating a local poll to cost around £250,000, and a national poll, more than £1 million. In practice, therefore, Deliberative Polls are beyond the reach of most public sector bodies.

Because of the costs involved in conducting Citizens' Juries and deliberative polls, the methods have been adapted in various ways to make them more affordable. For example, participants can be recruited by volunteering rather than through formal recruitment methods, the process can be shortened to two days rather than four, and much of the work can be done by staff from the commissioning body rather than researchers. These shorter events have been termed 'Community Conferences'. For example, in 2000 the London Borough of Lewisham was considering restructuring its library services by closing down smaller local libraries, and concentrating resources in a few large, well-resourced libraries. The council wanted to consult with local residents on this issue, and they convened a two-day 'Community Conference' to do so. They recruited a cross-section of the population from their Citizens' Panel and held a Community Conference, attended by about 70 members of the public and various council officers. The attendees were given a presentation about the options for Lewisham's libraries, including opinions from various professionals, and then put in small groups to consider the issues. In order to avoid people concentrating on their local area, the small groups were structured to include residents from different parts of the borough. As a result of this deliberative process, a consensus was reached that it was better to keep local libraries open even if this meant spreading resources more thinly, as libraries were important community facilities and not just hi-tech information centres.

On-going Approaches

Whilst deliberative methods aim to overcome the problems of uninformed responses to complex issues, panels have been used to develop on-going relationships with people over a period of time. Whilst panels have long been used in commercial research, they have usually been quantitative and have rarely been used as a relationship-building mechanism. In the public sector, the use of quantitative panels is now common – the government in the UK has a People's Panel, a representative sample of 5,000 people set up in 1998, and many local authorities also have panels. The advantages for quantitative research are that once the set-up costs are met, a panel is a relatively quick and cost-effective way to track changes in people's views over time. It can also be used to recruit specific sub-groups for other activities, such as the Community Conference mentioned above.

Qualitative panels are also used by public sector organisations in a variety of different ways, some aiming to recruit a representative cross-section of the general public, whilst others rely on self-selection among more specialist audiences. Those involving the general public tend to be more research-focused with a primary emphasis on data collection, whilst those involving specific audiences are usually more consultation-based, making little claim to representativeness but focusing on involving people in decision-making and holding policy-makers to account.

General public panels are usually recruited by formal recruitment methods to reflect the profile of the population. They are commonly used in the health service, where they are sometimes called 'health panels' (Richardson 1998). A typical health panel as described by Richardson involves 12 members of the general public chosen by quota sampling, who meet three times a year to discuss a topic chosen by the health authority. Topics might include prioritisation of services, for example whether older people should be offered expensive treatment even if the chances of recovery are low. Panel members are given information on the costs of treatments and how many people are affected, and are asked to consider the issues and arrive at a consensus. Panels may also vote on the issue, and if a large number of panels are convened this may give some indication of the weight of opinion (though this is clearly not as representative as a deliberative poll).

User groups are another common way to access public opinion about particular services, and also to create a relationship between the service provider and the user. This might involve users of social services, mental health services or housing, for example. In practice, these are often biased by self-selection – people are recruited on the basis of volunteering or responding to an advert – but if recruited more formally, they can be more representative. The difference between user groups and panels is that a user group meets with the senior management responsible for delivering the service, not with a researcher. They can then express their concerns directly to the management, and managers can try out new ideas and get early warning of problem areas. User groups, like client contact programmes in the commercial sector, can help put managers in closer touch with their 'customers', but the difference in the public sector is that people frequently have a legal right to the service and therefore to influence its delivery.

Special interest groups, or forums, are also common in the public sector. Often they are a way to gain the views of minorities who might be missed out, or just not noticed, in more general consultations. As pointed out earlier, the commercial sector can ignore minority concerns, but the public sector has a duty to make its services accessible to everyone. Thus, local authorities may meet with special interest groups claiming to represent, for example, such sections of the population as pensioners, ethnic minority communities, gay men and lesbians, and people with disabilities.

The advantage of meeting with specialist groups – people who run community organisations or provide advice, for example – is that they frequently have experience and expertise which is lacking within the commissioning body or indeed the research agency. Thus, they can advise on how the issue in question might impact on the community they work with, and can also assist in recruiting members of the community for further consultation. This can provide a useful compromise between the demand for inclusivity, which is central to many public sector consultations, and the real world constraints of time and budgets (see Desai and Sills 1996b for a discussion of this approach among ethnic minority groups, for example).

The most obvious weakness of these approaches is their lack of representativeness. Participants are frequently recruited through self-selection – volunteering, effectively – and this is likely to bias the sample in favour of people with a special interest, who may not be typical of the general population. Also, community groups who claim to represent a particular section of the population may not in fact do so, presenting partial views influenced by local politics, community factionalism or religious affiliations. And even when properly recruited, the small size of panels and the possible attrition as people drop out over time is likely to limit their claims to representativeness, although they do provide a high level of involvement and dialogue.

Area Forums

Area Forums were developed in the UK in the late 1990s as a way to re-engage local people with their local councils. Although gaining the views of the public is a starting point for the process, Area Forums are not princi-pally research exercises. Rather, they are an attempt by local authorities to relate to residents within the natural geographical boundaries of the local community (Lovell and Henderson 2000). The idea behind the area forum is that people will be more interested in getting involved if they believe that the issues relate to their local area, rather than larger strategic issues.

In January 2001, the London Borough of Southwark launched its Area Forums. According to *Southwark Life*, the council magazine, the intention was to 'bring together people who live or work in an area to discuss things that matter to them and to start to make a change' (*Southwark Life*, June/July 2001). The process so far has been as follows.

- The existence of the forums was advertised in various places, includ-ing the council magazine delivered to each household, inviting people to express an interest.
- Those who expressed an interest were invited to the first meeting of the whole borough forum. This was attended by several hundred people and was run as a large workshop, with people divided into groups to identify key themes, and plenary sessions to bring together people's contributions.
- The most important themes to emerge from the first full meeting – crime, and the environment – were then discussed at local meetings for each area. Council staff attended these meetings as well as other relevant organisations, such as the police. People were given key facts about the issue as it related to the whole borough, and then as it related to their specific area.

- The issues were discussed and action needed by the next meeting of the local forums was agreed.
- Each of the local forums was to report back to the full forum, which meets quarterly, to bring together local concerns at a more strategic level.

The advantages of Area Forums are that they offer the opportunity to get involved in and have some influence over strategic decision-making whilst also maintaining the relevance of these issues to local communities. The meetings are public and open, and therefore staff and councillors can be held to account for their decisions, and they are a long-term form of public involvement. On the other hand, they are clearly unrepresentative of the whole population and require a great deal of commitment from the public. Lovell and Henderson (2000) report that the forums set up in Barnsely have been dominated by community activists and older residents, aged 40–65. Thus, the high level of involvement offered by this method is not matched by a high level of representativeness.

COMMERCIAL APPLICATIONS

The IPPR report that in their Public Participation Awards for the year 2000, they did not receive a single entry from a commercial organisation. They concluded either that these methods have not been adopted by the commercial sector, or that companies are unwilling to publicise the fact if they are using such methods. Indeed, it could be argued that the priorities of commercial companies are fundamentally different from public bodies. Commercial companies are under no moral or social obligation to provide products or services – they do it in order to make a profit for their shareholders, and ultimately they are accountable to their shareholders, not their customers. They might also argue that whilst governments can and should reveal details of their activities and plans, commercial companies would damage their competitiveness if they did the same.

However, if corporations claim to act responsibly, to have a sense of involvement in their local communities, and to take account of public opinion when making investment or product development decisions, surely there might be a greater role for these consultative methods. This might involve some risk on the part of the company – it is always possible that a better informed public might be more critical – but the risk might well be worth it in terms of the insight the company would gain. A few examples are presented below where the commercial sector might benefit from using these approaches.

- Citizens' Juries might be very useful for commercial organisations involved in controversial areas, or subject to public criticism. For example, manufacturers of genetically modified foods might benefit from informed public opinion on their activities, rather than knee jerk reactions from surveys or lobbying from special interest groups. Similarly, the issues at stake in the recent 'anti-globalisation' protests – against the increasing power of multinational companies and their allegedly poor employment practices – would be ideal material for a Citizens' Jury or deliberative poll. One can only wonder what public opinion would be if consumers were told about the wage levels, manufacturing practices, environmental impact and profit margins of some global brands, and also given time to reflect upon the implications of changing these. Currently, manufacturers often defend themselves on the grounds that consumers purchase their products and therefore, implicitly, approve of their practices. Their position would be much stronger if they could demonstrate that a *fully informed* public would behave in the same way.

- Qualitative panels are still relatively rare, although they might be helpful in a range of applications. Their use in product development was referred to in the previous chapter, but they might also be used much more widely in service companies. If consumers were genuinely allowed to set the agenda for the sessions rather than respond to the client's priorities, organisations such as banks, insurance companies and telecommunications providers might gain a clearer picture of their customers' views and needs. And if customers were given direct access to senior management, they might have a real impact on corporate practice.

- Trade-offs and consensus-building could also be employed by commercial companies when considering the different options available to them for brand development. For example, they might want to cut down their brand portfolio in order to concentrate marketing effort on a few major brands. This could mean that some consumers' favourites would no longer be made, but other brands might be better promoted, more widely available and more profitable. In this case, it might be valuable to bring together consumers of the different brands and outline the options to see what they would do, as well as conducting more conventional group discussions to assess the impact of such decisions.

This is not to suggest that these strategic decisions should be made by consumers – clearly that would be impracticable. And the majority of consumers will not have been through the consultation process and therefore will continue to act according to their existing level of knowledge. However, there is a strong argument that companies would be in a better position to make these decisions, and to defend them in public when taken to task, if they were prepared to use more participatory methods to explore likely public reaction and priorities.

CONCLUSIONS

Qualitative research methods are extensively used in the public sector and their popularity is likely to increase over the next decade. This is driven by a variety of factors, including legislative requirements, a new consumerist approach to public services and concerns about people's lack of engagement in the political process. Many research agencies are used to operating in the commercial world, but the demands of the public sector can be different. Qualitative research in the public sector is an exciting new area, which allows researchers to talk to people who are often excluded from commercial research – either by design or by default – and challenges researchers to find new ways to engage with the public beyond the traditional researcher–respondent contract. However, there are different assumptions about the role of research in the commercial and public sectors, and there is a real need for mutual education and dialogue between clients and researchers. There are interesting possibilities for qualitative researchers to apply public consultation methods to commercial research problems, although these opportunities appear not to have been taken up. Methods such as Citizens' Juries, consumer conferences and qualitative panels have as yet been little used by commercial companies, which perhaps are reluctant to hand over too much power to the consumer. However, it is my belief that they offer real potential to access a more informed consumer opinion – a potential which as yet remains largely untapped.

KEY POINTS

- An increasing amount of research is being conducted by public sector bodies, including local and central government. This is driven partly by legislative requirements, but also by shifts in public expectations and the introduction of 'consumer thinking' into government.
- Qualitative methods are increasingly popular in the public sector, as they are considered more involving and engaging than quantitative surveys.
- There are several important differences which commercial researchers need to be aware of if they are working in the public sector:
  o There is a need to include a more diverse range of respondents, as public services have an obligation to serve everyone.
  o The issues involved are complex and it is important to gain an informed response rather than a knee jerk reaction.
  o Conflicting interests need to be reconciled and it can be important to arrive at a consensual solution.
- Research in the public sector is often conducted as part of a consultation exercise. In these cases, there is an expectation that participants will be told the results, and will have an on-going involvement in the decision-making process.

- Specific methods have developed to meet the different needs of public sector organisations, including Citizens' Juries, deliberative polls, user panels and area forums. All these methods share certain key features:

  o They provide people with information about the topic under analysis.
  o They allow people time to consider the issue and form an opinion.
  o They hold the decision-maker directly accountable to the participants.

- Researchers and commissioning bodies are frequently unclear whether they are engaged in a consultation exercise or a research exercise. In a research exercise, data collection is the main objective, whilst in consultation there is a need to develop an on-going relationship between the participants and the commissioning organisation.

Semiotics and Cultural Analysis

This chapter outlines the uses of semiotics and related methods of cultural analysis in commercial qualitative research. Whilst most qualitative methods involve direct contact with the consumer, semiotics and cultural analysis aim to interrogate consumer culture and marketing communications directly. This chapter begins by outlining the theoretical ideas upon which these methods of analysis are based, principally structural linguistics, cultural anthropology and the theory of consumption. It then goes on to outline how these ideas have been adapted in practice to explore the meanings of advertising, packaging, branding and other forms of marketing communications. Finally, some of the potential problems involved in using cultural analysis in qualitative market research are discussed.

Chapter 1 reviewed the various criticisms levelled against conventional qualitative market research methods. Interviews and group discussions, it has been suggested, rely too much upon the consumer and upon the idea that he or she is self-aware, self-determining and can tell us about their drives and motivations. Different approaches to the consumer within ethnography, creative workshops or public consultation have been outlined, but all these methods still assume that the consumer – whether ethnographic subject, creative partner, or empowered citizen – is at the heart of the research enterprise, and that qualitative market research must involve direct contact with the consumer.

Within semiotics, however, a different approach is taken. The consumer is not viewed as an independent, self-determining agent, making his or her own choices. Rather, consumers are viewed as products of culture, constructed and largely determined by the popular culture within which they live. Consumer needs, wants and desires are not the result of freely made individual choices, but rather a reflection of the surrounding cultural discourses. Thus, semiotics focuses the researcher's attention away from the consumer and towards the cultural context, including both popular culture and the marketing context. A conventional qualitative researcher might ask themselves, 'Why does Jane buy Timotei shampoo?' A semiotician would be more likely to ask, 'How does consumer culture give meaning to Timotei, and what are these meanings?' They might argue that if we can answer these questions, we will be able to make a good guess not just at why Jane buys it, but also why anyone buys it. This is because its meanings are constructed within popular culture, and consumers are influenced and constrained by this cultural context. This understanding of the broader cultural context is something that semiotic analysis is uniquely well placed to provide, because it focuses on the culture and not just the consumer.

The remainder of this chapter is divided into two sections. The first considers the theoretical background and outlines the ideas upon which semiotics and cultural analysis are based, while the second looks at practical examples and how these methods have proved useful in analysing advertising and branding. The reader will note that many of the examples draw on the work of Virginia Valentine and Monty Alexander, joint founders of Semiotic Solutions, a London-based consultancy which has pioneered the use of semiotics in UK market research.

THEORETICAL BACKGROUND

Cultural analysis in qualitative market research draws on a mix of theoretical traditions, including semiotics, structural anthropology and consumer theory. These diverse resources have proved useful to the analysis of popular culture and branding, and this combination has provided an eclectic conceptual toolkit used by qualitative researchers. Although often referred to by researchers under the blanket term of 'semiotics', for the purposes of our introduction, it is useful to separate the different theoretical traditions underpinning the approach.

Structural Linguistics

Semiotics, structural anthropology and consumer theory all have their origins in structural linguistics. Don Slater (1998) has described the history of semiotics, and this present discussion follows the framework he outlines. Structural linguistics is based on the theories of the nineteenth-century Swiss linguist Ferdinand de Saussure, who was interested in how language functions as a system, and how words come to have meanings in particular contexts. Saussure's theory contains several key ideas that are relevant to understanding semiotic analysis.

- **Words have no intrinsic meaning:** according to Saussure, individual words have no intrinsic meaning, nor do their meanings derive from the intentions of the speaker – they only acquire meaning in particular contexts. Thus, if I produce the sound made by the letters c – a – t, and you think of a furry four-legged small animal which meows, this is not because of any inherent properties of the sound, nor is it because of my

Intention. The relationship between the sound and the meaning is arbitrary.

- **Words acquire meaning through context:** the meanings we attribute to words are a function of the particular context, in this case the English language. Within particular contexts, it is conventionally accepted that the sound c – a – t will refer to the idea of a cat, and that is why you think of a furry animal which meows.
- **Language is a system of signs:** Saussure referred to these arbitrary relationships between sounds and meanings as signs, and suggested that languages are best understood as systems of signs. Saussure distinguished between individual words (*parole*) and systems of language (*langue*). He said that to understand any individual word, it was necessary to understand the entire system which gave it meaning.
- **Language produces reality, not vice versa:** Saussure's theory implies that language is not a transparent window on objective reality. Rather, language is a reflection of an arbitrarily chosen way to divide up the world, and this affects how we see the world. Other cultures will use different sign systems, and will therefore see the world in a different way. Although language systems appear to be natural reflections of the realities we see, in fact they are cultural constructions which give us a particular vision of the world.

There are three important concepts based on this theory of language which are central to semiotics:

- **The signifier:** this is the arbitrarily chosen sound which is used to bring to mind a particular concept – in the example above, the sound produced by the letters c – a – t.
- **The signified:** the concept which is brought to mind by the signifier – in this case, the idea of a cat.
- **The discourse:** the discourse is the overall context within which signifiers come to have meaning – the English language, in this case.

Some researchers use the term 'code' to refer to the relationship between the signifier and the signified. Thus, c – a – t is the code for a small furry animal within the context of the English language. They sometimes also go further and say that the concept of a cat is encoded in the sound c – a – t, and that when we hear the sound we decode it to retrieve the concept of the cat. As we will see later, ideas of encoding and decoding are central to the semiotic analysis of advertising, packaging and other areas of the marketing mix.

All these ideas have been very influential on semiotics as used by commercial qualitative researchers. We can analyse the language or discourse of brands, the cultural conventions of advertising and packaging, and the ways in which the discourse of the brand or category constructs a certain version of the reality, and implies a certain type of consumer. All these points will be discussed and illustrated in greater depth in this chapter.

From Structural Linguistics to Semiotics

Semiotics developed from structural linguistics by applying Saussure's theory of language to other areas of culture. There are many contexts which can be seen as sign systems similar to language, where conventions apply about how certain values, beliefs or ideas are communicated. For example, nightclub fashion, car advertising, shampoo packaging, hairstyles, body language, architecture – all can be analysed as sign systems, with conventions about the relationship between signifiers and signifieds. If the researcher can identify the discourse and its conventions, he or she can decode the meanings conveyed by specific adverts, packs, hairstyles, or whatever.

Let us return to our Timotei shampoo example, and explore how a semiotic approach might ask different questions from a conventional consumer-centred approach. A conventional qualitative researcher might conduct group discussions among purchasers, using various projective techniques to uncover the brand image. He or she might find that the green lid is associated with nature, the smooth bottle evokes shiny hair, and smallish size suggests a combination of treat and convenience. A semiotic analysis would want to reconstruct the system within which these signifiers and signifieds – the 'codes' of shampoo packaging – acquire their meaning. The semiotician would look at the whole system of shampoo packaging, finding perhaps that blue implied sports and quick washes, white was associated with luxury, or ribbed packs associated with activity and masculinity. Having reconstructed the whole system, the semiotician could analyse the position of Timotei in relation to other brands. He or she could also explore the implications of dividing up the world of shampoo in this arbitrary, culturally specific fashion. He or she might decide that the discourse of shampoo makes it easy to associate femininity with luxury, but less easy to associate it with physical activity. He or she might therefore suggest that if the client wanted to position a new product as both active and feminine, they would need to introduce a signifier outside the existing discourse – a different colour or pack shape, for example. A semiotic analysis could also help develop this new pack, to ensure that all the signifiers worked in the same direction and to avoid confusing the consumer. For example, a pack that was both ribbed (activity/ masculinity) and white (luxurious/feminine) might be semiotically confusing, whilst a white pack with a more dynamic illustration might avoid invoking these conflicting codes. And all this could be done by analysing the meanings of the signifiers within the shampoo discourse – 'decoding' the packs – without consulting the consumer.

Clearly, then, a semiotic approach can be very helpful in developing and evaluating marketing communications, as it provides a set of analytical tools whereby individual executions and whole communications programmes can be systematically analysed. In particular, semiotics can help with:

- Mapping out a new market or a whole field of cultural activity.
- Seeing the opportunities for new brand positionings.
- Analysing how different aspects of marketing communications work together, and synergising activity across different media.
- Evaluating in-store retail developments and harmonising the different aspects of marketing communications.
- Diagnosing problems with brand or marketing communications.
- Providing models and guidelines for successful brand communications, indicating the key signifiers within the relevant context.
- Understanding the process of encoding and decoding more precisely, to minimise the potential for misunderstanding between marketer and the consumer.

(Adapted from Semiotic Solutions website: www.semioticsolutions.com)

Structural Anthropology

Saussure's theories of linguistics have been very influential in the field of structural anthropology, particularly as practised by the French anthropologist Claude Lévi-Strauss (Lévi-Strauss 1962, 1964). Lévi-Strauss applied the principles of structural linguistics to the analysis of cultural systems rather than language systems. He drew particularly upon Saussure's idea that individual components of any cultural system (*parole*) had to be understood in the context of the whole system (*langue*). He developed his ideas in three key areas relevant to commercial researchers.

- **Deep structures:** Lévi-Strauss believed that human societies were influenced by deep, underlying cultural structures. He felt that surface cultural phenomena – rituals, kinship, myths, classificatory systems – were driven by much deeper underlying structures which people themselves might well be unaware of. He believed that the role of the anthropologist was to uncover these deep structures, by looking for patterns in the surface phenomena which would reveal the underlying forces. These deep structures were also thought to be intrinsic to the human mind and possibly universal, cutting across cultures to reveal the essential structure of mind and society.
- **Binary oppositions:** structural anthropology is also based on the idea that deep structures revolve around binary oppositions. Individual terms are not to be understood in isolation, but rather in relation to what they are not, in the context of the overall system. Thus, Lévi-Strauss felt that human cultures were structured by deep oppositions, such as male/female, right/left, sacred/profane and clean/dirty. Once again, the tendency to classify the world into oppositional structures was seen as inherent to the human mind.
- **The role of myth:** Lévi-Strauss felt that the role of myths was to help reconcile these deep structural oppositions, and to resolve the

contradictions and conflicts which they created within individuals and societies. The study of myths, he felt, was a valuable way to access deep structural oppositions, and he spent much of his career gathering myths from around the world and analysing the oppositional forces which they seemed to contain. Lévi-Strauss felt that in spite of the variations, changes and inversions between individual myths, all myths reflected these underlying cultural oppositions which lay deep in the human mind.

Lévi-Strauss' ideas have proved particularly useful for understanding consumer cultures and reactions to brands, which in many cases do seem to be structured by cultural oppositions – individual and society, freedom and constraint, safety and danger, for example. His analysis of myth has also proved fruitful in the analysis of advertising, and in exploring what have been termed 'brand myths'.

Consumer Theory

The final area of theory relevant to cultural analysis in qualitative research is consumer theory, which explores the cultural meanings of consumption (Valentine 1995; Glaros 1997). It explores what is happening when we consume, what we are consuming and how the act of consumption is given cultural meaning. Semiotic analysis focuses principally on marketing communications and bases its interpretation on the meaning of the signifiers within the relevant context. Consumer theory looks at how these semiotically encoded meanings are decoded by the consumer, and the relationship with the brand which is established through this encoding–decoding process. Consumer theory argues that consumption is not merely an economic activity. It is also a cultural activity, and when we consume we are purchasing not only products but also cultural meanings. Indeed, the identity of the consumer is seen as constructed through the act of consumption, via the meanings encoded in the brand. Brands offer consumers particular forms of identity – positions within the brand discourse – and consumers may accept, reject, or renegotiate these meanings. By analysing the various subject positions created in the brand discourse, and matching these against consumer needs and desires, the researcher can make a reasonable guess at the most productive target audience for the brand. We can relate this to the idea of contextual identities, discussed in Chapter 2. Let us take an example to see how this might work in practice.

When a consumer encounters a brand in context – say, a bottle of Timotei on a shampoo fixture in a supermarket – the relevant brand discourse is activated in the consumer's mind. This allows the consumer to decode the meanings of the brand, so that she knows Timotei is associated with nature, gentleness, femininity and shiny hair. In semiotic terms, this is the 'preferred reading' – it is what the brand wants the consumer to think, the position which the brand consumers for itself within the discourse. However, the brand discourse also constructs a position for the consumer, by making assumptions about their desired identity, aspirations and needs. Indeed, Virginia Valentine (1995) has suggested that the brand allows the consumer to construct a new identity for herself by accepting the position offered by the brand discourse. This is what is meant by saying that consumer identity is constructed by the act of consumption. If the position offered by the brand is meaningful, relevant and appealing, then the consumer will accept it, and the relationship with the brand will be stronger. If it is not, the consumer may reject the brand, or may purchase the product in spite of the brand discourse: 'I'm not a blonde passive woman, but I do like the shampoo.' Clearly, however, it is best if the brand offers an appealing subject position for the consumer, and the product delivers on the brand promise. Thus, consumer theory analyses the subject positions created within the brand discourse, and gives the consumer a more active role in accepting, rejecting, or negotiating these brand meanings.

THE USES OF SEMIOTICS AND CULTURAL ANALYSIS

Semiotics, structural anthropology and consumer theory provide an eclectic analytical toolkit for analysing brands and marketing communications. They draw upon a range of theoretical perspectives, all of which derive in some way from structural linguistics. And they are all based on two key ideas:

• Cultural messages are encoded and decoded within particular contexts.
• By analysing the individual manifestations of culture, we can gain insight into the underlying structures which they reflect.

The remainder of this chapter shows how these methods have been used by commercial qualitative researchers to explore three main areas:

• Advertising and marketing communications as sign systems.
• Consumer cultures and their structures.
• Brands and advertising as forms of narrative, or myth.

Marketing Communications

Semiotic methods have proved most powerful in the analysis of visual data, particularly advertising executions, packaging and overall retail design. These different areas can all be viewed as sign systems functioning in a similar way to language. Within each discourse, there are conventionally accepted relationships between signifiers and signifieds. The signifieds – the values that brand owners want to communicate – are encoded within the signifiers – colours, shapes, logos – and the consumer can decode these meanings because of the shared conventions of the discursive context.

Let us imagine we are conducting a semiotic analysis of the meaning of Timotei shampoo. Monty Alexander's article 'Codes and Contexts' (2000) provides useful guidelines as to how we would do this. Bearing in mind the principle that signifiers only acquire meaning as a consequence of their context (the discourse), our first task is to identify the relevant context. In practice, this can be quite difficult, as brands clearly exist within many contexts simultaneously. Our bottle of Timotei shampoo may be placed within the context of other shampoos, but it could also be placed within a wider context of hair care, or health and beauty products. And of course the entire health and beauty category may be placed within the wider context of a supermarket.

Our choice of context needs to be guided by the purpose of the analysis, but Monty Alexander suggests that the category or brand context is a good starting point. Depending on which element of the marketing mix we are looking at, we may also define the context by media – thus, one context might be television advertising, another might be packaging. Let us assume we are looking at the semiotics of the pack and the television advert, and the relationship between the two. Our task is to trace the particular examples back to the overall sign system. This will tell us the scope of the discourse, what the discourse 'allows' us to say about shampoo and what it inhibits. We would need to gather together a range of examples of Timotei packaging and television adverts, current and historical, and also examples of competitive marketing activities. This would almost certainly involve analysing features such as colours, shapes, textures, typographies, pack sizes and images on the labels. For the television adverts, we would conduct a similar analysis of shampoo advertising, looking at features such as camera angles, music, characters represented, clothing and social situations, and relating them back to their meanings within the discourse of shampoo adverts. From this, we could analyse the systematic relationships between specific executional features and values or cultural meanings. When we had done this, we could be said to have 'decoded' the discourse of shampoo marketing – we would understand more precisely how and why particular brands communicate particular messages, and we would understand this for the entire category, not just Timotei.

This sort of analysis is clearly very useful for a variety of reasons. It allows marketers to see exactly where their brand lies in the context of the competition, and the extent to which it uses codes that are common in the category, or more distinctive semiotic strategies. It can identify which elements of the marketing mix are working well and which are not, thus diagnosing potential problem areas. It can be very helpful in harmonising brand communications across different elements of the marketing mix. For example, Gordon and Valentine (1996) point out that whilst TV advertising is a very active medium, packaging changes much less frequently.

The codes of the two areas of brand discourse may therefore become out of alignment, with TV using more up-to-date codes, and packaging lagging behind. This analysis is also valuable for in-store redesign work. In supermarkets with a range of different categories on sale, semiotic analysis can uncover potential conflicts between categories. Consumers need time to shift from one discursive context to the next, but if conflicting categories are placed right next to each other consumers may become confused. This may result in people rushing through the category, or purchasing the most familiar brand as a way to minimise confusion. Semiotic Solutions conducted a design audit for Safeway supermarkets, analysing all aspects of the in-store communications to help Safeway shift from a 'middle class' top-up store, to a mass market family supermarket. Their audit enabled them to advise Safeway on the promotions and merchandising which would encode the appropriate messages within the context of supermarket shopping.

Harvey and Evans (2001) provide a very interesting example of the use of semiotic methods by the Added Value Company, a UK marketing research consultancy, to decode advertising messages in the international beer market. Guinness wanted to understand their competitors' advertising propositions so that they could design their own strategies to be distinctive and competitive. They commissioned AVC to conduct a semiotic analysis of global beer advertising, and to advise them on how they could conduct their own semiotic analyses of competitive advertising in the future. AVC first gathered together examples of television advertising from around the world, and conducted a semiotic analysis to identify what the competitors were communicating and how they were doing this. They uncovered a range of signifier–signified relationships, which they grouped around key themes, such as individualism, sexual relationships, cosmopolitan style, etc. Thus, they mapped out the entire discourse, identified the key themes within the discourse, and grouped the signifiers and signifieds around these themes. This enabled them to isolate the 'codes of masculinity' within beer advertising, or the 'codes of individualism', i.e., the way in which these values are conventionally encoded within the discourse of beer advertising. On the basis of this framework, they felt able to analyse the communications content of competitive advertising by breaking down the executions into their key components, and mapping these signifiers against the relevant signifieds: 'decoding competitive advertising propositions', as the title of their paper suggests.

Use of Structural Analysis to Understand Consumer Culture

Structural anthropology, as we have outlined, is related to semiotics in that it looks at specific cultural forms – myth, ritual, relationships and language, for example – as manifestations of underlying structures which give rise to them. Like structural linguistics, the idea of context is important, as specific aspects of culture are not to be understood in isolation but rather in an overarching cultural framework structured according to deep-rooted binary oppositions. However, it does differ from semiotics in that there is rarely a clear signifier–signified relationship. Structuralist analysis looks for broad patterns which may sometimes be coded in specific contexts – fairy tales or myths, for example – but frequently show themselves in thematic similarities across different cultural arenas. In traditional structural anthropology, researchers were looking at entire cultures and trying to uncover universal human values, but in market research our aims are usually more modest. According to Monty Alexander (2000), a semiotic analysis of marketing communications is often useful to combine with a similar analysis of the relevant areas of what he terms 'popular culture', in order to relate the position of the brand to the trends in consumer culture. This can allow the researcher to assess whether the brand is lagging behind, firmly in the mainstream, ahead of the game, or simply irrelevant to consumer culture.

As with the selection of the relevant context for analysing marketing communications, deciding which areas of consumer culture to focus on can be difficult. The final decision is likely to be based on experience and intuition, but the two most likely starting points are the activity or the target audience. So for Timotei, one would look at popular culture as it related to hair care, or one might look at the popular culture relevant to the target audience. Assuming we had decided to focus on popular culture and hair care, we might want to analyse sources such as.

- News articles and reports about hair care or new treatments.
- Women's magazines, both general and health- and beauty-focused.
- Films and television programmes, looking at hairstyles of the stars, or representations of washing or styling hair.
- Representations of hair in advertising for other product categories.
- Popular songs.
- Fairy tales, folklore and myths, e.g. Lady Godiva, Rapunzel.

In analysing these forms of popular culture, we would be looking for patterns, themes, repeated ideas and taken for granted assumptions about the role and importance of hair. We might explore the representations of bald people in the media, look at stories or films representing the trans-formative effect of hair cutting, and at how different hair styles are associated with different personalities and characteristics. We could then attempt to relate our findings in popular culture back to the brand communication and marketing discourse, to see how the two compared. Returning to Timotei, we might find that the brand was positioning itself as 'natural' using rather dated signifiers – meadows and waterfalls – whereas consumer culture may have moved on to 'organic' signifiers, represented by rainforests and South American tribes. Or we might find that attractive women in films are now more likely to have short hair, semiotically coded as dynamic and empowered, whilst the flowing blonde hair of the Timotei woman was associated with a passive, dated version of femininity. By tracking the consumer culture against the marketing codes, we could therefore recommend whether the brand might need revitalising – a semiotic makeover, so to speak.

Drawing on the work of the cultural critic Raymond Williams, Semiotic Solutions developed the concept of mapping cultural trends against the communications codes of brands (Alexander 2000; Alexander et al. 1995; Pryke et al. 1998; Semiotic Solutions website). Following Williams, they suggest that within every cultural framework, or discourse, there are three overlapping zones of culture:

- The residual culture, representing the past, outdated and often moribund culture.
- The dominant culture, representing the present, which is often hard to see because it is taken for granted.
- The emergent culture (of which there is frequently more than one), representing possible futures.

(Alexander calls these zones 'codes', but in order to avoid confusion with the use of code to identify the signifier–signified relationship discussed above, we shall refer to them here as zones of culture.)

They go on to suggest that semiotic analysis 'identifies and tracks the communication codes of the brand (and those of the competition) across the real-time frame of the surrounding cultures, in order to project future market developments that the brand can tap into'. According to Alexander, this mapping of brand codes against movements in the background culture is one of the most powerful contributions of semiotic analysis to marketing communications.

Pryke et al. (1998) used this framework in their analysis of the election of New Labour and its likely impact upon the world of marketing. They reviewed media coverage of various major cultural themes – gay rights, women's issues, youth unemployment, attitudes to the monarchy and to the death of Princess Diana – as well as conducting consumer research on attitudes to the New Labour government. The authors state that they began their research with the assumption that the election of New Labour heralded a new emergent culture. However, their cultural analysis and consumer research suggested that consumer culture had changed faster than political culture, and that the relative informality of the New Labour government was an example of politics catching up with the public, not leading it. Indeed, they suggest that one reason why New Labour was elected with such a landslide majority was that it slotted so neatly into the emergent culture of informality and loosening of respect for traditional sources of authority. It was a brand that was perfectly in tune with its time.

An example of a brand that was in tune with the dominant culture but needed to create a new emergent culture, is provided by Alexander et al. (1995) in their analysis of British Telecom's brand communications. BT wanted to encourage consumers to make longer telephone calls, and asked Semiotic Solutions to explore the 'cultural position of telephone chatting' in order to do this. Semiotic Solutions conducted cultural analysis and consumer research, and found a binary structural opposition underlying attitudes to telephone chatting. 'Big Talk', as they term it, constituted the male discursive world – rational, purposeful, important and necessary communications. This was opposed to 'Small Talk', the world of female communication, characterised as unimportant, trivial, emotional and unnecessary. This was evident through the language people used to discuss the issue, and was consistently expressed by male and female respondents. Within British telephone discourse, female modes of communication were downgraded, and BT's tone of voice in addressing the consumer colluded in this dominant culture. Thus, in terms of consumer theory, the brand communication activated a discourse of telephone chatting which constructed an unappealing and devalued position for the female telephone caller. This, clearly, was no basis to establish a meaningful brand relationship with female consumers, nor to challenge the dominant male telephone culture. BT realised that they needed to change their own tone of voice, and intervene in the dominant culture, to provide an appealing subject position for the female consumer within the brand discourse. The new advertising strategy, 'It's good to talk', was part of BT's attempt to raise the status of 'small talk' and help create a new emergent culture in the context of telephone use.

Brand Discourses and Brand Myths

We have pointed out above that brands activate discourses, and that these discourses provide subject positions for consumers. The analysis of brand discourses involves identifying the relevant area of discourse, and then identifying the subject positions it offers to the consumer. If these positions appeal to the consumer, their relationship with the brand is likely to be more meaningful. Consumer theory, often combined with semiotic analysis, helps us understand how brands provide relevant subject positions for consumers, areas where they fail to do this, and ways in which the semiotics of the brand communication could be adapted to offer more motivating positions.

   Gordon and Valentine (1996) provide some interesting examples of the relevance of category discourses and subject positions in their analysis of the semiotics of retail outlets. They explored the semiotics of supermarkets, garage forecourt shops and corner shops as different purchasing environments which offer different consumer identities. The supermarket, with its orderly aisles, large trolleys and well-stocked shelves, constructs a position for an organised shopper doing a weekly or fortnightly shop, probably knowing what they want to purchase before they go in.

The garage shop, with its emphasis on fuel purchase, suggests buying things while on the move. And the corner shop, with its 'higgledy-piggledy clutter', provides opportunities for impulse purchase and discovery, but also implies a less organised shopper, going out to buy things which they have forgotten, or run out of. Thus, these different outlets deploy different semiotic strategies which construct different positions for the consumer (clearly backed up by the range of products on offer). An analysis of how these subject positions are created, and how appealing they are to consumers at different times, could have important implications for merchandising, display and promotions, relevant both to the brand owner and to the retailer. For example, brand owners might offer different promotions to corner shops, taking advantage of the tendency to purchase on impulse. Retailers might develop different semiotic strategies for different parts of the store, or different branches – a 'shop and go' section for consumers who are not in 'organised shopper mode' within larger supermarkets, for example.

We have mentioned above that the analysis of myth is central to structural anthropology. Lévi-Strauss was interested in the forms of myths, the characters, narrative devices and plot lines which recur across different myths. He also suggested that myths are a way to reflect upon and resolve essential contradictions in the human condition – life and death, nature and culture, or man and god, for example. Alexander (1997: 87) suggests that this same analytical method can be applied to brands, stating that 'virtually every consistently successful brand today embodies its own particular myth'. By myth, he means the ability to reconcile a cultural contradiction which gives the brand its power. If the brand's 'root myth' can be identified and expressed, this provides insight into its power and longevity. For example, a recent poster for Volvo has the strapline 'safe sex' above a picture of a car, implying that the brand reconciles the desire for safety with the attractions of danger. Marks and Spencer ready meals reconcile the desire for high-quality food with the lack of desire to prepare and cook it. Wash and Go reconciles the desire to keep one's hair healthy and attractive, with the reticence to spend time leaving in conditioners. All these brands embody particular myths, they reconcile important cultural contradictions, and this, says Alexander, is the magic of the brand.

Virginia Valentine (1995) develops this further in her use of fairy tales to analyse advertising and brand communications, drawing on Propp's morphology of the folk tale. Propp suggested that fairy tales are characterised by stable, constant elements; that the characters serve a limited set of functions; and that the narrative sequence and essential shape of fairy tales are basically the same, regardless of their particular structures. Propp suggests that most fairy tales contain a villain, a hero, the donor of a magic agent, and a helper. The sequence of the fairy tale is that there is a lack of something, the hero and villain are identified, the magical agent is received, and the hero overcomes the lack and defeats the villain with the magic agent. As Valentine points out, there are frequently essential ingredients in the narratives of advertising, and this means we can analyse the formal structure and logic of adverts without worrying too much about their specific content. This structure could be helpful to identify exactly what lack the brand fulfils, how it does this, what the villain is, and what transformation the brand achieves. By applying this structural analysis to a range of advertisements within a category, we could identify the essential components of the category narrative, and assess whether particular brands offered anything distinctive or merely replicated the general category fairy tale.

Limitations of Cultural and Semiotic Analysis

Before concluding, attention should be drawn to some potential weaknesses in this form of analysis. Slater has suggested that although semiotics can be interesting and compelling, it is hard to describe it as a reliable or replicable method (Slater 1998). Although the analyst's interpretation may be insightful, there is little guarantee that any other semiotician would come to the same conclusion about the relevant codes or myth structures. Harvey and Evans (2001) assume that another group of semioticians would come to the same overall conclusion as they did, but they offer no evidence of this. In practice, it can be hard to select the relevant discourse to analyse, but this choice will clearly influence the semiotic interpretation of the brand's meanings. Also, it is not entirely clear how the semiotician arrives at his or her interpretation of the relationship between the signifiers and signifieds within a discourse. In many cases, it seems to rely upon the shared knowledge of the cultural background and upon intuition, which may be accurate, but is hard to validate. Also, the position of the consumer can be unclear in semiotic analysis. In principle, he or she is seen as passive, determined by culture and unable to break out of his or her contextual frame. However, consumer theory does go some way to remedying this by giving the consumer a more active role in interpreting, accepting or resisting the brand's semiotically encoded meanings. But if the consumer and the semiotician disagree over the brand meaning, it is not clear whose interpretation should be prioritised.

CONCLUSIONS

Semiotics and other forms of cultural analysis offer a radical challenge to a basic assumption of commercial qualitative research – that it requires some interaction with the consumer. Semiotics, structuralism, the analysis of myth and consumer theory allow the researcher to engage directly with consumer culture. They focus our attention on the mechanisms by which advertising, brands and products acquire their meaning, rather than on specific examples of those meanings. They can therefore be very effective al placing consumer responses within a wider cultural framework. They also foreground the process of qualitative analysis rather than the method – although it has been suggested that this reflects a lack of method within cultural theory and an over-reliance on the interpretation of the individual analyst.

KEY POINTS

- Semiotics and cultural analysis are based on the idea that consumers are constructed at least partly through culture, and therefore to understand the consumer the researcher must understand the cultural context.
- Semiotics is the analysis of the relationship between signs and their meanings, within specific cultural contexts. Semiotic analysis has proved useful in explaining the cultural meanings encoded in advertising, packaging and design.
- Structural anthropology is based on the idea that the surface phenomena of any culture reflect deeper underlying structures. Structuralist analysis has proved helpful in exploring consumer culture, drawing on materials such as media coverage, film and television, popular stories, myths, jokes and marketing communications.
- Consumer theory explores the cultural meaning of the act of consumption – what does it mean to a consumer when they purchase or use a particular brand? By analysing the assumptions built into the brand communication (the brand discourse), and the consumer identities which it creates (the subject positions), consumer theory can help explain how brands establish relationships with consumers.
- Although cultural analysis has provided considerable insights into the workings of marketing communications, its methods are hard to replicate or validate, and it relies heavily on the insights of the individual analyst.

Qualitative Research and the Internet

This chapter examines the impact of the Internet on qualitative research methodology. It starts by looking at the general difference between online and face-to-face communications, and goes on to describe the most common qualitative methods used online – online group discussions, Moderated Email Groups and bulletin boards. We continue by discussing various studies which have looked at the advantages and disadvantages of online qualitative research, and conclude suggesting that these methods are still at a relatively early stage in their development.

THE IMPACT OF THE INTERNET

The impact of the Internet upon a wide range of social, commercial and political arenas has been widely documented (Herbert 2001; Perrott 2000; Pincott and Branthwaite 2000). Among other things, the Internet is credited with bringing about changes to our perceptions of geography, of nationhood, of community and political organisation. The impact on the world of marketing has been great too, with scarcely a week going by without another conference about using the Internet for branding, advertising, or public relations. The advent of digital television, the convergence of telephone, Internet and television, and the interactive possibilities offered by these new technologies, have opened up new possibilities for relationships between corporations, or governments, and the public. A whole new field of research topics has also been created, including website usability, content requirements, interactivity, pricing, distribution and online branding (Dixon 1996; Gormley 1995; Pincott and Branthwaite 2000).

The Internet has also had a direct impact on the market research industry, presenting opportunities and threats. On the one hand, the instant and direct access which companies have to their customers might reduce the need for large research agencies, with their costly infrastructures of field controllers, interviewers, data processors and mail rooms. Companies can monitor site traffic and place questionnaires on websites themselves, and computer packages can produce the tabulations automatically (Comley 2001; Langer and Bunofsky 2001). However, the Internet could also offer solutions to many of the problems which beset the research industry. Researchers have commented on declining response rates, increasing public resistance to direct mail and telephone interviews, and the difficulties of recruiting over-researched samples such as business people and IT managers (Jack and Homans 2000). Using the Internet as a means of recruiting and gathering data might overcome these problems, putting respondents in control of the interaction – they can decide whether, when and how to reply, at a time and in a way convenient to them.

Regarding specific methods, the general consensus (Perrott 2000; Pincott and Branthwaite 2000; Walker 1997) is that the impact on quantitative methods has been considerable, and is likely to grow. The use of e-mail as a delivery method for questionnaires, which may be sent as executable file attachments or more commonly as a hyperlink, means that turnaround times can be dramatically reduced. Pop-up surveys can be conducted on websites, and computer software allows the results of self-completion questionnaires to be analysed immediately, without the need for time-consuming data entry. And questionnaire design can be more adaptable and flexible, thus offering real advantages over traditional methods.

The Internet as a data collection tool has also impacted on qualitative research, and groups have been conducted online since the mid- to late 1990s. However, the extent to which online qualitative research offers a real advance in methodology, as opposed to providing mainly practical benefits, is still being assessed. Qualitative research has traditionally relied upon direct contact between the researcher and the respondent, usually but not always face-to-face. One of the strengths of qualitative research has always been its use of group dynamics, non-verbal communication, body language and tone of voice, as integral parts of the data analysed. Certainly, few qualitative researchers would claim they could gain the same insights from looking at a transcript as they can from actually being present at the group or interview.

So, what is the role and status of online qualitative research? Is it merely, as suggested by some clients, 'a cheaper and slightly less effective alternative to traditional qualitative research' (Walker 1997)? Or does it offer real advantages which mean we might actively choose online over face-to-face methods? These are the questions this chapter will address. First, we will look at the differences between online and face-to-face interactions. Secondly, we will describe and compare key online qualitative methods. Thirdly, we will explore some of the key issues involved in conducting qualitative research online compared with face-to-face methods. Finally, we will return to the question of the status and role of online qualitative research.

ONLINE AND FACE-TO-FACE INTERACTION

The debate about the role of online qualitative research can be illuminated by briefly comparing it with other qualitative research methods. For example, when we compare group discussions and in-depth interviews, we are aware of the strengths and weaknesses of each method. We know what the key differences are in terms of dynamics, likely coverage and appropriate topics, and we choose our methods appropriately. Group discussions provide for more interaction, dynamism and creativity, and we would therefore be more likely to employ groups for creative development work. Depth interviews give us more individual detail, are better for exploring decision-making processes, and avoid the biases that may be introduced by the group context. Thus, most researchers would recommend the mix of methods that was most appropriate for the research topic and sample, rather than trying to conduct depth interviews in a group, or generate group dynamics in an individual interview.

Online qualitative research, however, has only recently been viewed as a different, specific form of interaction, with its own advantages and disadvantages. This is partly because of the history of online methods, which started with conducting group discussions online, i.e., in a chat room context. As Nicky Perrott has pointed out (2000), this constituted an attempt to transfer an existing method – the group discussion – into a new medium – the Internet. Thus, it is perhaps not surprising that the jury is still out on the real methodological benefits of doing this. Much of the debate about online groups (e.g. Herbert 2001) has revolved around trying to demonstrate that 'cyberqual', to use Michael Herbert's memorable word, can deliver more or less the same outputs as conventional, face-to-face group discussions. And much energy and thinking has been expended on how to bring the online group nearer to a 'real' group, in terms of the tone and content. However, when online groups are judged by the same criteria as face-to-face groups, it is almost inevitable that they are found wanting in some way – they lack a sense of interaction, the researcher does not gain 'insight', it is hard to get a clear picture of the individuals in the group (Coates and Froggat 1998; Herbert 2001; Jack and Homans 2000; Langer and Bunofsky 2001). Under these circumstances, conducting online groups can be justified on two grounds.

- First, it can be argued that although the interaction online is not as full or lively as it would be in a face-to-face session, the method still produces valid and reliable data so the lower level of interaction is not important.
- Secondly, the practical benefits of online groups outweigh the (slight) methodological disadvantages, i.e., in real terms the choice is not between online groups and face-to-face groups, but between online groups and no groups at all.

Nevertheless, it seems inevitable that if online groups are assessed by the same criteria as face-to-face interactions, they will always be seen as a slightly less effective version of 'real' groups (Walker 1997). This does not mean, however, that online groups are not valuable methods of data collection with very real benefits, which should be the method of choice for some studies. However, it does suggest that they will be chosen for their practical benefits, rather than for any methodological advantages offered.

More recently, several researchers have begun to reconsider the methodological benefits of conducting qualitative research online, and have argued that we should exploit the particular characteristics of online interactions rather than trying to replicate face-to-face interactions (Adriaenssens and Cadman 1999; Beasley and Chapin 1998; Coates and Froggat 1998; Eke and Comley 1999). Online interactions have three key differences compared with face-to-face:

- The medium is text rather than speech.
- The researcher and respondent are not in the same physical place.
- The interaction can be more flexible and does not need to be in real time.

These characteristics could be seen as potential benefits to be exploited, rather than problems to be overcome, offering a different sort of inter-action which might prove suitable for some topics or target audiences. Building on Pincott and Branthwaite's analysis (2000), the following characteristics distinguish online from face-to-face communications.

- Intimacy can be established quite quickly compared with face-to-face interactions.
- Online respondents tend to be more self-absorbed, because they are usually alone, meaning that they may spend more time responding.
- E-mail communications can be more considered, formal and thought-out, because of the text-based medium.
- They can also be more light-hearted, informal or casual in other contexts.
- Opinions can polarise, with people tending to express more extreme views than they would in a face-to-face conversation.
- Online communications lend themselves to playfulness, games and fantasy.
- The Internet offers a democratic, sharing, anti-commercial environment, where social hierarchies can be suspended.
- The Internet can be associated with illicit subjects or forms of communication, perhaps due to the apparent anonymity offered.

Clearly, then, the different characteristics of online communications might make them more suitable for certain subjects and target audiences, offering researchers the ability to do things they could not do in face-to-face interactions. However, whether the researcher is conducting online groups, e-mail forums, using bulletin boards or some other hybrid methodology, these differences will need to be taken into account in deter-mining the best use of online methods.

QUALITATIVE ONLINE METHODS

This section outlines the main qualitative methods used in online research, and provides examples of some case studies where they have proved useful.

Online Groups

Online group discussions were among the first uses of the Internet for qualitative research, pioneered in the UK by Michael Herbert Associates. An online group attempts to replicate a conventional group discussion, using web-based chat room technology. As with a conventional group discussion, six to eight respondents are recruited and invited to log on to a password-protected chat room where the discussion takes place. Because of the range of tasks that need to be carried out – reading the responses, typing questions, ensuring stimulus materials are correctly used, responding to client contacts – often two moderators conduct the group, although they will appear as the same person to the respondents. A range of software tools have been developed to customise the format for qualitative research, such as the ability for client and researcher to communicate without the respondents' knowledge, the ability to launch new browsers on the respondents' computers, and the ability for the researcher to communicate by e-mail with individual respondents when necessary. Frequently, although not always, online groups are conducted to test new websites, and therefore it is common for the respondents to be asked to visit a site for a few minutes during a group, and then return to the chat room to give their reactions. Whilst as yet the quality of video clips viewed over the Internet is not good enough for research, it is possible to send CD ROMs for respondents to view during the group.

A good example of online group discussions is the research conducted by Jeff Walkowski (2001) of QualCore, a US qualitative research consultancy, for Motorola. Motorola wanted to develop their websites which provided information about semi-conductor products to design engineers. The websites contained a huge amount of technical information about many different products, and Motorola wanted to make the sites more user-friendly. Walkowski decided to conduct online research because the target audience was geographically very dispersed, and also because he thought the use of a new interesting research method would motivate engineers to take part. There were also budgetary considerations, and the fact of having immediate transcripts available was appealing. The consultancy chose online groups over bulletin boards because they wanted spontaneous, immediate reactions, rather than more considered views. Respondents were recruited from lists supplied by the client, using telephone methods in order to maximise response rates. Walkowski says that the respondents had no trouble expressing themselves online, and that the groups gathered valid and reliable data, shown by the fact that responses were consistent over a range of online projects that were conducted.

Bulletin Boards

Bulletin boards can also be used for online research, although apparently they are more common in the USA than the UK (Eke and Comley 1999). Bulletin boards are a Web-based technology, where respondents are invited to log on to the board once a day. The moderator posts questions and the respondents can post replies at their convenience, as in a news group. Everyone can see everyone else's comments and can follow the threads of discussion of individual questions. A new question is posted every morning, and the moderator reviews the answers at the end of the day.

Casey Sweet (2001) of Quesst Qualitative Research, a US-based consultancy, conducted a project using bulletin boards for the College of Veterinary Medicine at Michigan State University. The project aimed to explore attitudes among teachers and consultants towards a particular aspect of veterinary practice management, in order to guide the development of academic programmes. Sweet chose online methods because the sample was geographically dispersed and comprised busy professionals. Bulletin boards were chosen for several reasons. First, the project required respondents to consider detailed information, read stimulus materials, and respond in a thoughtful manner. Secondly, the target audiences comprised two clear 'communities' – consultants and teachers – and a 'community-based' methodology allowing the two groups to interact among themselves was thought likely to encourage participation. Two bulletin boards were conducted over a 5 day period, with respondents recruited through the university. The groups comprised 25 consultants, of whom 21 participated regularly, and 19 teachers, 14 of whom participated, with a core group of 5–7 participating regularly. Sweet concluded that the method was well adapted to involving busy professionals who were interested in the field, but might find it difficult to attend a group discussion at a fixed time, whether on or offline.

Moderated Email Groups

Email forums, or Moderated Email Groups,* are a relatively new development, and seem to offer the possibility to overcome the problems associated with bulletin board methods while maintaining their benefits. Moderated Email Groups take place over a week or two, with the moderator e-mailing questions to respondents who then e-mail their

---

*Moderated Email Groups is a registered trademark of Virtual Surveys Limited.

responses back to the moderator. After each set of questions and answers, the moderator produces a summary of responses which is sent to the group for their comments, along with further questions. The main distinction between this method and bulletin boards is that the researcher has a greater degree of control over the discussion, summarising and feeding back only the points which the moderator wants other respondents to see.

Adriaenssens and Cadman (1999) used Moderated Email Groups for their study of online share dealing. The target audience was upmarket shareholders who were also Internet users, a low penetration and hard-to-reach sample. Online methods were chosen because of the difficulties of recruiting group participants, and the desire that there should be some degree of interaction between respondents. Adriaenssens and Cadman do not specify why e-mail groups were chosen over online groups, but the method clearly offered them the advantage of providing a breathing space between waves, so they could consult their client on technical matters and also involve the whole team in deciding the course of the discussion. Two Moderated Email Groups were conducted, one comprising 20 active shareholders and one with 10 passive shareholders. They found that the method provided well-considered, valuable responses, that there was a greater diversity of response than might have been expected from face-to-face groups, and that respondents appeared to be very frank and honest with their views, especially when making criticisms. They do, however, point out that the opportunities for probing, clarification and genuine interaction are limited, and that the whole process requires a lot of executive time and administrative back-up.

Hybrid Methods

Hybrid methods, utilising quantitative and qualitative tools together, can also be better deployed online than in face-to-face groups. They are an interesting field, as they suggest areas in which the online medium allows researchers to do things that would not be possible face-to-face, rather than replicating a face-to-face session. Johnson and McKane (2001) provide an interesting example of the potential of this approach. They conducted online groups on two new product development projects – one on digital cameras and one on washing machines. In both projects, part of the research brief was to assess the motivational appeal of a range of specific features, in order to determine which were viewed as essential, which were likely to distinguish their clients' product, and which were not valued. They do not specify why online methods were chosen over face-to-face methods, although the implication of their article is that the opportunity to conduct a quite complex evaluation of product benefits was a key reason.

For the washing machine project, two online groups were conducted among women who had recently shopped for washing machines.

In addition to the standard discussion about attitudes, emotions and preferences, the session included a self-completion questionnaire in which respondents were asked to rate 28 product features. The software was constructed for the mini-survey to pop up at the appropriate point in the discussion, and the results were immediately calculated producing a list of ranked benefits. These could then be explored more fully as the group continued, looking at the reasons for particular preferences. Johnson and McKane suggest that the advantages of this method are that it provides a different way to evaluate what respondents have said in the group, it provides instant feedback on preferences and polarising issues, it is fun for respondents and adds variety to the session.

ONLINE METHODS: ADVANTAGES AND DISADVANTAGES

The next section of this chapter discusses the key issues to have emerged from the debates around online qualitative research. Various studies have been conducted comparing online research with face-to-face methods (Beasley and Chapin 1998; Eke and Comley 1999; Herbert 2001; Langer and Bunofsky 2001; Walkowski 2001), and the results of those studies are reviewed here. Following the structure offered by Michael Herbert in his review of pros and cons of online qualitative research (2001), it is divided into the following sections:

- Practicalities
- Sampling and recruitment
- Quality of data
- Veracity of data
- Analysis and reporting.

Before entering into the detail, however, it is worth pointing out that there does not appear to be a clear consensus on these issues. Many claims are made about the benefits of online research derived from quite small surveys among particular target audiences – design engineers, academics, or high net worth bank customers, for example – and we can only make tentative generalisations about how people respond to online methods compared with face-to-face.

Practicalities

The main advantages of conducting qualitative research over the Internet are often assumed to be practical. It is thought to be cheaper, quicker and more convenient than face-to-face interviewing. However, studies have found that this is not necessarily the case.

- **Cost:** it is often assumed that online qualitative research will be cheaper than face-to-face work, as there will be savings on travel, accommodation, venue hire and the like. However, in practice the additional costs involved in setting up the project and providing technical support, coupled with the increased demands on executive time, mean that the costs of online groups and face-to-face are usually comparable (Herbert 2001). One exception to this is in the United States context, where it is usual for a team of clients to attend groups. In these cases, it might indeed be cheaper to conduct the work online (Walkowski 2001).
- **Timings:** it is a moot point whether online methods are necessarily quicker than face-to-face research. On the one hand, according to Jack and Homans (2000), recruitment can actually take longer online, as respondents still need to be screened and checked by phone. However, at the other end of the project there may be time savings because transcripts are available for analysis immediately. Overall, however, it does not seem likely that speed of turnaround is a key benefit of online qualitative research except in certain limited circumstances. Indeed, using bulletin boards or Moderated Email Groups can take considerably longer than conventional group discussions.
- **Physical convenience:** the fact that the moderator, respondent and client do not need to be physically co-present during the research is a real advantage, particularly for respondents who are geographically dispersed, or when the client team may be international. The possibility for a large number of client observers to view the session without intruding can clearly be helpful for projects where this is required (Coates and Froggat 1998; Langer and Bunofsky 2001; Walkowski 2001). Also, some of the software used for online groups allows for a split screen so the client can communicate with the moderators without the respondents knowing this. Once again, US researchers have found this to be a real benefit, although Langer has pointed out that the ease with which clients can intervene needs to be controlled.

Sampling and Recruitment

These practical advantages of being able to bring together geographically dispersed populations has brought real benefits in terms of recruitment and sample construction, as outlined by various researchers (Adriaenssens and Cadman 1999; Eke and Comley 1999; Jack and Homans 2000; Sweet 2001; Walkowski 2001). These benefits include:

- **Easier to locate and recruit specialist samples:** Jack and Homans suggest placing pop-up invitations to take part in research on relevant websites, e.g. MP3 sites for young people, or car auction sites for motorists. Walker (1997) found that placing a message in a discussion group to take part in research on the technology transfer market, a very specialist field, yielded 18 eligible respondents within a single day.

- **Easier to recruit very busy people:** because the Internet is a more democratic medium than, say, telephone conversations, it can be easier to recruit target audiences such as business people, IT managers, or others who are difficult to recruit over the phone. This is because e-mail messages are less intrusive, and people can respond in their own time.

- **Better geographical spread within samples:** because respondents do not have to be physically co-present, online methods can cover a wider geographical area. This is advantageous for all research topics, as it will increase the representativeness of the sample, but can be essential for projects focusing on low penetration samples or those which are geographically dispersed. For example, Adriaenssens and Cadman (1999) conducted two e-mail groups among individuals who dealt in shares and used the Internet, clearly a low penetration sample. And Walkowski (2001) conducted several online groups for Motorola among engineers who designed products using semi-conductors, clearly a target audience who would be almost impossible to recruit to a face-to-face group discussion.

- **More diverse samples:** because social class hierarchies are reduced on the Internet, it is possible to include a wider range of respondents within a session. According to Adriaenssens and Cadman (1999), this is especially true of e-mail forums, where respondents do not interact directly with each other. For example, one might include students, part-time and full-time workers and also retired people in the same sessions, whereas face-to-face this might be difficult.

It has also been pointed out (Walkowski 2001) that because online groups and e-mail forums are a new and 'sexy' research method, this alone might motivate respondents to take part. Particularly for young people who are used to chat rooms, people working in IT or early adopters of technology products, the chance to take part in an online discussion could be an interesting offer.

However, many researchers have found that recruitment cannot be conducted entirely over the Internet (Coates and Froggat 1998; Walkowski 2001), as the 'no show' rates for such online recruitment methods are far higher than for conventional methods. The level of emotional commitment offered by e-mail is not the same as that provided by face-to-face or telephone contact, and most researchers suggest that respondents recruited over the Internet should be confirmed, and re-screened, by telephone. Even doing this, however, drop-out rates for online methods are usually higher than for face-to-face methods. Whilst it is easier to take part in an e-mail forum or online group than a face-to-face session, it is also easier to drop out without feeling guilty.

Finally, of course, there is the issue of the representativeness of samples recruited over the Internet. Whilst the penetration of the Internet is growing rapidly, in the UK in 1999 it was still only around a third of the population (NOP Internet user profile), and there are wide differences by age and social class. Also, of course, participation in online research requires typing skills, and a reasonable level of literacy and facility with technology, which not everyone has. Thus, whilst one may be able to construct reasonably representative samples of some specialist audiences – professionals, business people, academics – the use of online methods for general public samples will still exclude a large proportion of the population.

Quality of Data

Much attention has been paid to the quality of the data provided by online research. In most cases, this is viewed in comparison with face-to-face methods, although as we have suggested above, some researchers are now looking at exploiting the different nature of online communications. There have been several studies designed to compare the data gained from different methods. Most of these have compared online groups with face-to-face groups (Beasley and Chapin 1998; Herbert 2001; Walkowski 2001), although some have also included bulletin boards and e-mail forums (Eke and Comley 1999; Langer and Bunofsky 2001). However, different researchers have arrived at different conclusions about data quality, and there is no clear consensus on this issue. We will look at this under three headings:

- Reliability of data
- How respondents express themselves
- How respondents interact.

Reliability

This is one area in which there is a broad consensus on comparisons between online and face-to-face methods – when they are conducted on the same topics, the same basic findings emerge. There is no evidence that the online medium prompts people to say different things, make up things which are not true, or assume attitudes which they would not express in face-to-face groups. Also, the findings from different online groups on the same subject demonstrate a reasonable degree of consistency, suggesting that they do provide a valid and reliable means of gathering data (Beasley and Chapin 1998; Eke and Comley 1999; Herbert 2001), with the proviso that the data one wishes to gather concerns attitudes, experiences and behaviour, rather than emotions and feelings.

How Respondents Express Themselves

In online research the moderator does not have access to the usual cues by which he or she evaluates what respondents say. Tone of voice, body language, facial expressions and other audiovisual cues are all absent from the online environment. This can make it difficult for researchers to feel that they have understood and empathised with respondents as real people. Some researchers have suggested that although they have understood the words, online groups do not provide them with real 'insight' into respondents' feelings and motivations (Beasely and Chapin 1998; Langer and Bunofsky 2001).

Nevertheless, because respondents know that these cues are absent, there is some evidence that they try to compensate for this. For example, Walkowski shows how his respondents – who were technologically sophisticated design engineers – used capital letters and exclamation marks to give the appropriate tone to their words. And Beasley and Chapin suggest that respondents use language more carefully in order to convey feelings which they cannot convey through body language. Indeed, they contrast the 'well-constructed sentences' of online respondents with the 'hesitations and non-sequiturs of speech' (1998: 200). Herbert found that respondents encountered few difficulties expressing themselves online and did not feel inhibited by the medium.

Various researchers have observed that responses in online groups tend to be shorter than those in face-to-face groups (Beasely and Chapin 1998; Herbert 2001; Langer and Bunofsky 2001). Interestingly, Langer and Bunofsky's analysis found that the total number of responses per respondent was similar, that is, that respondents were having the same number of opportunities to 'speak', but each of their utterances was shorter. This had led to a suggestion that online responses are shallower than those gained in face-to-face groups. However, as Herbert points out, the issue is not the length but the quality of response. People cannot type as fast as they speak, and there is also a time pressure in an online group to make your response quickly before the discussion moves on, so it is not surprising that responses would be shorter. The question is whether they manage to express themselves more succinctly, or whether there are things they wanted to say which they have had to leave out. Both Herbert (2001) and Beasely and Chapin (1998) imply that responses are merely shorter, not lower quality, but neither provides sufficient evidence to assess their claims. And in contrast, Anne Ward, Director of Qualitative Research at IPSOS in the UK, suggests that there are problems of expression for 'ordinary respondents' who may not have such fast typing speeds, or may simply be less familiar with computer technology.

There seems to be a consensus building that the quality of responses from bulletin boards or e-mail groups tends to be high. In part, this is because the data is being judged on its own merits and not compared with face-to-face methods. In these forums, people have time to respond at their convenience, they can consider their views and opinions, draft and edit their response, and send it when they are happy with it. Indeed, some researchers have been surprised at the time and commitment participants are prepared to dedicate to these methods (Adriaenssens and Cadman 1999; Eke and Comley 1999; Sweet 2001). Indeed, Eke and Comley suggest that the quality of response they received from Moderated Email Groups was actually better than they would have got from conventional groups or depths, or from online groups. This is an interesting example where the textual basis of online communication, requiring a more considered response, was seen as a positive advantage rather than a problem needing to be overcome.

How Respondents Interact

Group interaction is clearly one of the main benefits of conventional groups, giving the moderator the chance to cross-fertilise ideas and explore one person's comments among the whole group. The evidence of group interaction in online groups and e-mail forums or bulletin boards is unclear, although the most common conclusion seems to be that although it can occur it is by no means inevitable and is always limited. Langer and Bunofsky, for example, found little evidence of interaction in their online groups, feeling that respondents were 'fairly oblivious to what others were saying' (2001: 7). The client also commented that there was little evidence of 'give and take' in the online group, and that respondents seemed to be concentrating on reading and responding to the moderator's comments rather than paying attention to each other. In contrast, Beasley and Chapin (1998), and also Herbert (2001), found that respondents did interact between each other in their online groups. Herbert points out that respondents do attempt to convey their personality through humour and banter, and Beasley and Chapin comment that respondents frequently remain online chatting to each other after the moderator has signed off, suggesting that they did indeed 'form' as a group. Michael Herbert has also suggested that the style of moderation can also be key to generating high levels of respondent involvement (personal communication).

Another issue with online groups is the difficulty following the discussion. Because people type at different speeds, and because everyone can type their response at the same time, the order of responses can become jumbled. One respondent may be answering the previous question, when the discussion has moved on to a different topic. Or they may be replying to something 'said' earlier but the sequence may be interrupted by another comment. This can make it difficult to follow the discussion, and Herbert reports that it was a real cause of frustration for some respondents.

With bulletin boards and Moderated Email Groups there is less opportunity for respondents to interact with each other. Although in theory on a bulletin board all respondents can read each other's comments, bulletin boards frequently generate so much information that it is hard for respondents to do this. Eke and Comley (1999) point out that respondents may not bother to post their comments if they can see someone else has already said the same thing, whilst Sweet (2001) found that if there were a lot of comments respondents tended to restrict themselves to answering the moderator's questions without generating much discussion between themselves.

In e-mail groups, interaction between respondents is controlled by the moderator. The respondents do not communicate with each other, nor do they always know who the other respondents are. Rather, they e-mail their comments to the moderator who collates them, and circulates the summary to all the respondents for their comments. This has the advantage of giving people a summary rather than expecting them to trawl through all the comments, and may therefore encourage a greater degree of interaction. The three studies that have looked at the role of Moderated Email Groups are inconclusive on this issue. Two of them suggest that interaction is limited (Adriaenssens and Cadman 1999; Eke and Comley 1999). However, Jack and Homans (2000) found a greater sense of interaction could be generated if respondents had already attended a face-to-face group, and Adriaenssens and Cadman found their participants adopted a more informal style when they had previously spoken to them on the phone. This suggests that the quality of online interaction is substantially enhanced if combined with some offline interaction as well.

Finally, it has been suggested that online groups, bulletin boards and Moderated Email Groups are more democratic, and that it is difficult for any one respondent to dominate (Adriaenssens and Cadman 1999; Eke and Comley 1999; Herbert 2001; Langer and Bunofsky 2001). With online groups, this may relate to the fact that people cannot talk over each other. If one person wants to dominate, that does not prevent others from typing and posting their comments. With MEGs, each respondent replies to the moderator's questions without knowing what others are saying, so there is clearly no possibility to dominate, nor can respondents be influenced by each other's comments. It has therefore been found that online methods can generate a greater range of responses and diversity of opinion than face-to-face methods – perhaps a benefit of the limited respondent interaction.

Veracity of Data

There are two potential issues concerning the truthfulness of data gained from online research:

- It has been suggested that respondents give more open, frank and honest replies when online, as they are not worried about offending others or about addressing embarrassing topics (Eke and Comley 1999; Herbert 2001; Walkowski 2001).

- And it has also been suggested that responses might be less honest, because people can assume false identities more easily when online, which would be harder to sustain face-to-face.

Although these might appear contradictory, they both relate to an essential feature of online communications – the sense of distance, even anonymity, between the people communicating. Essentially, the question is how people respond to this new aspect of communication; they might take advantage of it to speak their minds, or they might adopt false identities and invent new personalities for themselves.

Various researchers have suggested that online communications show a greater degree of honesty than face-to-face methods, particularly when it comes to criticising products or disagreeing with others. Some of Herbert's younger respondents felt more at ease disagreeing with other respondents online, but overall they felt they had been honest both online and face-to-face. Herbert has also conducted online groups among teenagers for a project developing a drug education website, where he felt that the anonymity offered by the medium encouraged young people to be more open (personal communication). Walkowski (2001) shows that his design engineers were perfectly happy being harshly critical of Motorola's website online, whilst Adriaenssens and Cadman (1999) felt that their respondents were particularly candid in their Moderated Email Groups. Eke and Comley (1999), interestingly, suggest that sensitive topics such as the use of pornography on the Internet might be more frankly addressed in online research, perhaps because of the lack of social pressures which characterise face-to-face groups.

Problems with respondents claiming false identities have not been noted in the research papers reviewed, although it is recognised as a potential problem. Bearing in mind that recruitment for online research usually includes some offline screening, such as telephone interviewing, the problems associated with online research are not necessarily much greater than those involved in any qualitative research. Also, this is probably less of an issue for specialist samples, which are often the topic of online research. It is quite easy to pretend to consume one brand of coffee rather than another, but it is much harder to pretend to be a design engineer, a consultant veterinarian, or an IT manager. Herbert (2001) suggests that 'it is easier for people to stay in their own roles than invent alternate ones', but he does acknowledge that if respondents want to deceive the researcher, it is easier to do so online than face-to-face. And if more online work is conducted among the general public, experience suggests that the opportunity for cheating will not go unnoticed.

Analysis

Online methods can speed up the data analysis of qualitative projects. After an online group, the moderator has an immediate, full transcript in which all quotations are attributed to individual speakers. Respondents type their comments when taking part in either bulletin boards or Moderated Email Groups, so this makes it easier to cut and paste quotations into the final report. And people's written comments are easier to read than typed up transcripts of verbal conversations. This may seem a relatively prosaic benefit, but some moderators have clearly found it very helpful. Indeed, both Beasley and Chapin (1998) and Coates and Froggat (1998) describe this to be the single most compelling benefit of online methods. Coates and Froggatt suggest that they can produce complete reports 'within a couple of days of the group' (1998: 193) because of the high-quality data which is immediately accessible.

However, without wishing to dismiss the obvious practical benefits, it does seem that this position is overstated and based on a limited view of the contribution of online methods to the analytical process. Clearly, one can review the data more quickly because it is immediately available, there is less of it, and it is easier to read than a transcript of a conventional group. Thus, the sorting of the data can be done more quickly and efficiently. However, there is no obvious reason why the researcher would spend less time interpreting the meaning of online data than any other data. Anne Ward from IPSOS suggests that 'it is quicker if you believe respondents say what they mean' but if you want to dig beneath the surface 'it's not much different from face-to-face data'. Also, it would be a dangerous precedent if online research came to be seen as intrinsically quicker or easier to analyse, as the absence of non-verbal communication and the jumbled order of comments may actually make it more difficult to interpret.

CONCLUSIONS

Thus, online group discussions do offer real practical benefits, but there is still a desire to replicate real life interviewing online – and as long as this is the case, online methods will always be seen as second best compared with the 'real thing'. As yet, qualitative researchers have made limited progress in developing genuinely new methods which exploit the particularities of online interaction, rather than trying to minimise their effects.

There are signs of developments in this direction, with Moderated Email Groups and bulletin boards building on the advantages of the Internet to develop new research tools. Rather than trying to overcome the text-based nature of online communication and the lack of interaction, they use these features to gather more considered, thoughtful and individual data. They use the flexibility of e-mail to allow people to take part as and when they wish, and they allow a more iterative, developmental approach to qualitative data analysis. There are also some interesting examples of hybrid methodologies, combining online discussions with limited real time quantification.

Nevertheless, the potential of the Internet remains far from fully exploited in qualitative market research. Moderated Email Groups and bulletin boards might be appropriate for a whole range of technical or professional audiences, as well as topics that are highly sensitive such as criminality or sexual abuse. Equally, qualitative research has not yet found ways of utilising key qualities of online communications – playfulness, anonymity, illicit activities, assuming new identities – and the long-term impact of the Internet on qualitative methods remains to be seen.

KEY POINTS

- The Internet has made a strong impact on quantitative research methods, although its impact on qualitative research has been less far-reaching.
- The different characteristics of online communications make it possible to conduct qualitative research in different ways:
  - The medium is text rather than speech, lending itself to more considered opinions.
  - The researcher and respondent do not have to be in the same place.
  - The research can be conducted over a longer time frame because the cost implications of repeat interviewing are much lower.
- The main online methods used in qualitative research are:
  - Online group discussions, which attempt to replicate conventional groups within a Web-based chat room environment.
  - Bulletin boards, where the researcher posts a question and respondents log on throughout the day to post their responses.
  - Moderated Email Groups, where the researcher sends the questions to the respondents, receives the answers and produces a summary of responses which can then be sent out again to form the basis for subsequent questions.
- New hybrid methods are developing which exploit more fully the uniqueness of online research methods, such as including quantitative questionnaires which can be administered online during the group.
- The practical convenience of online methods allows researchers to access geographically dispersed samples, specialist groups or very low penetration target audiences, giving real benefits in sample construction and recruitment.
- The anonymity of the medium means that a greater diversity of respondents can be included in individual sessions, and also that responses can be more varied.

- Online methods appear to produce reliable and valid data which is comparable with face-to-face methods. However, online groups can produce more superficial responses and lower levels of respondent interaction.
- Bulletin boards and Moderated Email Groups can produce high-quality data, as respondents can reply in their own time and often dedicate considerable time and thought to composing their responses.

Conclusions

This book has outlined the criticisms that have been levelled against conventional, interview-based research methods. Some of these criticisms – such as the link between what people say and what they do, and the relationship between interviewer and interviewee – are longstanding concerns within sociological debate. Others – such as the extent to which conventional qualitative methods can assist in processes of innovation – have been driven by recent changes in the marketing context. Some commentators have even argued that conventional methods should be all but abandoned (Earls 2001; Pillot de Chenecey 2000), whilst more sympathetic writers (Gordon 1999b; Smith and Dexter 2001; Spackman et al. 2000) have suggested that a radical re-think of the role of market research is required. Gordon has suggested that we should re-invent ourselves as 'pro-searchers' and should focus on 'innovative ways of searching out information relevant to the future'. Spackman and his colleagues claim to have identified an emergent new paradigm, which they term 'informed eclecticism' or 'bricolage'. Smith and Dexter comment that many writers have been arguing for a 'radical new approach to market research' (2001: 183).

So, what does our survey of recent developments in qualitative research tell us about the status of these claims? Is there a case for a radical overhaul of market research, and a new paradigm to unite our efforts? Or are we dealing with a series of evolutionary changes, building upon current practice and broadening our range of activities? The material discussed in the preceding chapters certainly suggests that qualitative market researchers are broadening the range of their activities, and also that research buyers are asking researchers to engage in different sorts of task. They may want us to generate new ideas, provide insight into cultural trends, or facilitate direct contact with the consumer. Alternative methods have been developed to address these needs, and in many cases this new thinking can be combined with existing methods, rather than replacing them.

This chapter argues that there is little evidence of or need for a 'radical new approach' or 'paradigm shift' within qualitative research. The philosophical underpinnings of qualitative research, including assumptions about how we gain knowledge (epistemology) and what we can learn about (ontology), may need to be refined, but not rejected. The questions researchers ask to assess the reliability, validity and consequent status of data – how and why was this data generated, what biases might there be in it, how representative is it, what is its context?' – still make sense. However, researchers do need to broaden the range of data to which these principles can be applied, and change their ways of working – not paradigms or philosophies – in order to address the changed marketing context and consumer. There is indeed a need for a 'set of easily accessible guiding principles that can be shared and built upon', (Smith and Dexter 2001: 191), but as they suggest it would be an error to search for a 'grand theory' of market research.

This chapter describes six areas where important changes can be seen in the world of qualitative research. Bearing in mind what we know from Chapter 3 about the inherent uncertainties involved in prediction, the possible impact of these changes on qualitative research in the future is suggested. The chapter concludes by constructing two alternative scenarios, and leaves the reader to decide which is the more likely.

The six most important shifts in the future of qualitative research are likely to be:

- From talk to action
- From reporting to experiencing
- From respondents to partners
- From understanding to innovation
- From interviews to eclecticism
- From data to insight.

FROM TALK TO ACTION

The psychotherapeutic interview was developed to access feelings, attitudes and emotions. It was concerned with uncovering people's interpretations of their situation, and, via the process of exploration with the therapist, coming to an understanding of why the client behaves as he or she does. The method was never really envisaged as a way to explore actual behaviour – to find out what people really do, how they react to stimuli, and how they behave in specific social contexts. Groups and interviews are now frequently used to explore behaviour, but what we access via interviews is reported behaviour, not the behaviour itself. Interviews are usually distant in both time and space from the behaviours they are trying to understand – researchers take people away from the context of their actions, and ask them to report events, feelings or behaviours which took place in the past.

However, the shifts in the marketing context outlined in Chapter 1 mean that relying on interview data alone is likely to become less and less satisfactory. We have described the growth of retailer power, the importance of category management and the focus on the whole consumer experience rather than on individual brands or products. There is also the increased desire of brand owners to associate their brands with lifestyles, to gain respect and credibility among cynical consumer groups, and to manage more closely the total 'brand experience' in the retail environment. All these trends require a deeper understanding of social and cultural context. The minor details of the marketing mix which are processed at low levels of involvement will become all the more important to understand purchasing decisions at the point of sale, but interviews are not the best way to research these issues. This will require a greater use of observational and ethnographic methods, including video observations in store, accompanying groups of consumers to a range of social events, and spending longer periods of time with smaller groups of people. It will also suggest that the shift away from approaches derived from psychology and psychotherapy, towards anthropology and cultural studies, is likely to continue.

FROM REPORTING TO EXPERIENCING

Much of the work reviewed suggests that the shift towards clients' having a more direct, experiential involvement in research projects will continue and become more important. The traditional model of the researcher taking the brief, going away and coming back weeks later with the results is likely to become less common, as clients will increasingly value direct contact with the consumer. First-hand experience can make a stronger impact, be more memorable and spread insights more quickly and powerfully through an organisation than reading research reports or hearing presentations. In principle, this is a very positive trend. The growth of Consumer Connection programmes demonstrates that these are found to be valuable by many retailers and manufacturers. They increase the confidence of the marketers' decision-making and also the respect marketers have for and the understanding they have of their consumers. Nevertheless, it is very important that these consumer contacts are managed by skilled researchers, and that clients are given the necessary skills, training and debriefing to gain the maximum value from such sessions. In the absence of a proper training and debriefing programme, the best case is that random insights are captured by individuals but not spread through the organisation. The worst case could be inappropriate interpretation of idiosyncratic consumer comments, and decision-making that might be more confident, but based on poorly understood and unreliable information.

FROM RESPONDENTS TO PARTNERS

Conventional interviewing tends to keep respondents in the dark about the real purposes of research. The term 'respondent' defines the role of the interviewee as reactive and passive – they respond to the researcher's questions and to the stimulus materials. They are rarely given information about the client's needs, the marketing problem or the underlying advertising idea, because researchers have been worried that this might affect their responses in ways that would invalidate the research. However, if respondents are now postmodern, cynical, marketing-literate consumers, we may no longer need to protect them from the fact that there is a marketing plan and advertising strategy, and that they are part of it. They probably already know and, if they are under the age of 25, they may have studied marketing and advertising at college.

Indeed, as discussed in Chapters 3 and 4, there can be very real benefits in treating research participants as partners in a problem-solving process, rather than as passive respondents. This can help to democratise the unequal power relationship which characterises normative interviewing, providing participants with information about the research problem, with time to consider the issues and with direct access to the decision-makers. We can also talk to people repeatedly rather than insisting on one-off interviews, allowing them to develop their own insights as the research progresses. This can provide richer data, greater commitment from participants, and more useful, actionable outcomes for clients. For projects where innovation is the desired outcome, or for public sector work where the development of a relationship with participants is important, this more collaborative approach can yield real benefits.

However, this approach is not suitable for all projects and for all respondents. Not all members of the public are cynical consumers waiting to be amused by the next advertising message, nor are all young people familiar with the language of marketing. There are still real risks of biasing responses if we tell people what marketers' intentions are before we explore their spontaneous reactions. And any serious involvement of the public, whether as consumers or citizens, in more collaborative approaches needs careful preparation so that people know what is expected of them, and have the time, commitment and understanding to take part effectively. Indeed, one of the failings of much public consultation is that it asks people to participate in processes that can be quite stressful and time-consuming, but it does not provide the support needed to take part meaningfully. Consumer research risks failing in the same way if we believe that a collaborative approach can be reduced to telling people what the marketing strategy is and asking for their views, an approach that is not completely unheard of, and sometimes suggested by inexperienced clients. Thus, whilst a shift in the nature of the relationship with the respondent is important and helpful for some projects, it needs careful management and thought, and cannot simply be bolted on to a more conventional research approach.

FROM UNDERSTANDING TO INNOVATION

Linked to this changing relationship with the consumer is a change in the outcomes demanded from qualitative research. Traditionally, the role of qualitative research in creative and new product development projects has been evaluative. The advertiser, marketing people or NPD agency come up with several new ideas, and qualitative research is conducted to assess consumer reactions to the ideas. Discussions among the target audience are used to explore whether the product is likely to appeal, the creative executions meet the brief, and whether the desired brand values are communicated. The role of the consumer and the researchers has not been to come up the ideas, and indeed researchers often stress to their clients that 'respondents' cannot be expected to invent new products – they can only respond to the ideas with which they are presented.

More recently, however, qualitative researchers are being asked to help generate new ideas, come up with creative concepts, or develop new products, rather than simply gain consumer reaction to ideas created by the client team. The desired outcome is not a better understanding of the present situation, but rather a potential good new idea for the future. And as we have discussed in Chapter 4, conventional qualitative methods have not been developed with idea generation or creativity in mind. Thus, alternative methods may be necessary to meet clients' needs for innovation, such as brainstorming, creative workshops, sequential recycling, and new product development panels. As discussed, all these tasks use key qualitative research skills, and researchers can and should be involved in such activities. Qualitative researchers' ability to manage group dynamics, think through metaphor and analogy and hold several ideas in their minds simultaneously are all valuable for idea generation. Nevertheless, it is important to distinguish processes that aim to facilitate innovation from more conventional research processes. A brainstorming session or creative workshop uses many of the key skills of qualitative research, but it is not a research method. Rather, it is an example of how qualitative skills can be used for a range of purposes other than research. As long as the division between creation and evaluation is maintained, qualitative researchers may enhance their value to clients by engaging in these related activities; but if the line is blurred, researchers will find it hard to generate good creative ideas, or evaluate them reliably.

FROM INTERVIEWS TO ECLECTICISM

In the qualitative interview or group discussion, the data is discursive – what people said – and the analysis is based primarily on the words. Researchers pay attention to issues such as tone of voice and body language, but the primary form of data remains the verbal record of the interview, whether this is a tape recording or a transcript. Thus, a single method is used and a single form of data is prioritised. This is largely a consequence of the psychological origins of qualitative market research in the UK, where the aim has been to understand the attitudes and motivations of the individual, rather than to focus attention on the social and cultural context which might inform those attitudes.

However, various authors (Ereaut and Imms 2001; Gordon 1999; Smith and Dexter 2001; Spackman et al. 2000) have suggested that this narrow methodological focus has ruled out other sources of data which could provide richer, additional insights. This shift is related to the increasing use of frameworks and methods from anthropology and cultural studies, which focus on culture and society, as opposed to psychological or psychotherapeutic frameworks, which focus on the individual or the small group. A more eclectic approach, it is argued, would allow the researcher to develop the best way to research each issue, selecting data sources, methods and theoretical frameworks which are most appropriate to the task in hand. Commercial research agencies have tended to avoid this approach, but within academic qualitative research it is quite uncontroversial. For example, Denzin and Lincoln, in their *Handbook of Qualitative Research* (2000), describe the qualitative researcher as follows:

> The qualitative researcher as bricoleur ... uses the aesthetic and material tools of his or her craft, deploying whatever strategies, methods or empirical materials which are at hand. If new tools or techniques have to be invented, or pieced together, then the researcher will do this. (Denzin and Lincoln 2000: 4)

Thus, eclecticism covers both research methods ('strategies') and data ('empirical materials'). It has also been suggested (Ereaut and Imms 2001; Gordon 1999a; Spackman et al. 2000) that eclecticism includes the ability to select the most appropriate theoretical perspective according to the research problem. Thus, if one is trying to understand shampoo packaging, semiotic theory might be most useful; if the issue is how consumers notice point of sale materials, theories of low involvement processing might be best; and if we are trying to understand the key drivers behind the decision to drop out of school at 16 rather than continue in education, we might look at personality theories derived from psychology, as well as larger structural issues such as employment market trends.

In the author's opinion, the idea of using an eclectic mix of methods, data and theory is an important shift in how qualitative market researchers might view their role, practices and source of authority. As Gill Ereaut and Mike Imms point out (2001), it reveals to the commercial qualitative researcher a range of data from which we have artificially screened ourselves. If we adopt the approach of the bricoleur, we can generate new, vivid and compelling insights for our clients derived from analyses of newspaper articles, magazines, television drama, film, popular music, photography, fiction and other documentary sources, as well as interview data and observations. It also seems clear that such an approach would be more enjoyable for researchers to conduct, and for clients to see presented.

However, eclecticism or bricolage cannot be sensibly described as a new, or emergent, paradigm for research. The philosopher Thomas Kuhn, who developed the idea of the paradigm in the context of scientific research, describes a paradigm as a shared set of assumptions about how knowledge is acquired and how theory is developed (quoted in Lazar, 1998: 12). Thus, 'eclecticism' cannot be a paradigm as by definition an eclectic approach will not have a consistent body of theory or method, nor will all the approaches used share the same philosophical assumptions. Indeed, Spackman, Barker and Nancarrow (2000) point out that across the social sciences there is a move away from grand unified theories, towards the development of smaller strands of theory for specific areas of study. Empirically too, the shift to a more eclectic approach is a development of current research practice rather than a complete overhaul. Ereaut and Imms point out that most qualitative researchers would consider using a wider range of data sources for some projects, if there were good reason to believe that interviews or groups would not deliver the insights required. The issue, they suggest, is to reposition eclecticism at the centre of qualitative research, rather than on the fringes as a last resort – an evolutionary, rather than revolutionary, change.

However, there are real challenges for the commercial researcher who wants to take bricolage seriously as a research approach. Market researchers work for clients who have to take big commercial decisions, often involving large amounts of money and resources. These clients need to know, and believe, that the data upon which these decisions are based is reliable and robust enough to inform their decision-making. When single sources of data are used, such as group discussions or quantitative surveys, we have reasonably well-established ways to evaluate the data. On the other hand, as Smith and Dexter (2001) have observed, when multiple sources of data, generated in different ways with different levels of reliability, need to be integrated, things become more complex. We need to know how to interpret the different data sources, how they were genera-ted, what questions we can ask of them, and how we can assess their reliability and representativeness. But if we are analysing cultural arte-facts such as, say, the letters page of a men's lifestyle magazine, we are unlikely to have access to all the information we need to make that judge-ment. Thus, we need consistent ways to assess, analyse and interpret the range of data we use if we are to convince our clients that bricolage is a robust and reliable approach to research. Smith and Dexter suggest that, rather than a grand theory or paradigm, what we need is a consistent body of principles that outlines how professional researchers approach any data: what questions should be asked of it, and what criteria should be used to evaluate it. It is this area, rather than the development of grand theories or paradigms, which researchers should focus on If they are to place themselves at the centre of marketing decision-making.

FROM DATA TO INSIGHT – TWO SCENARIOS FOR THE FUTURE OF QUALITATIVE RESEARCH

Finally, there has been an important change in the way that clients assess marketing information. One sign of this is the shift away from the job title 'Market Research Manager' to 'Consumer Insight Manager' within what were previously called research departments. The role of a Research Manager is to commission robust, reliable, technically well-conducted surveys, and to suggest the implications of this research to marketing managers. Usually, a Research Manager will rely on the marketer to tell him or her what research is required, and is likely to be reactive rather than proactive. The role of an Insight Manager, in contrast, is to determine how and where meaningful consumer insight can best be gained and communicated to marketing managers. Conventional research would be one tool used, but the Insight Manager would also deploy a range of other approaches as appropriate, in the spirit of the bricoleur.

Clearly, this would also require a reassessment of the criteria used to judge the value of the research commissioned. The criteria conventionally used to assess research include:

- **Reliability and validity:** did it find out what it intended to, and is the data robust enough to inform the decisions that need to be made?
- **Replicability:** if the same study was done again, would it produce similar results?
- **Sample design:** did the sample achieved match the profile of consumers?
- **Quality of analysis:** was the data thoroughly analysed and accounted for?
- **Logical coherence:** does the analysis make logical sense and is it internally consistent?

While these criteria are still relevant, it is increasingly evident that this is not primarily how the value of research, or insight, is assessed. For the Consumer Insight Manager, the following questions might be more relevant:

- Was the research useful in helping decision-making within the company?
- Did it prompt change and did people act upon the findings?
- Did it provide new insights about the brand, product or service?
- Was it presented in such a way as to make an impact on the internal clients, i.e., marketing and brand managers?
- Did the research process provide the clients with a valuable experience of the consumer?

This trend is both a real opportunity for research to enhance its status and value to clients, and also a real threat to the research industry. If researchers can maintain high technical standards – even if clients are not interested in them – *and* extend their role further into decision- making, then the status of research within business could be considerably enhanced. On the other hand, if they abandon high technical standards, and rely solely on the usefulness of the outcome, researchers will lose their only real claim to uniqueness as researchers – a uniqueness which lies in their ability to handle and assess data according to a clear and reliable set of principles. Bearing in mind the difficulties with prediction outlined in Chapter 3, let us conclude by constructing two alternative scenarios for the future of qualitative research.

In the **Charlatan** scenario, there is a very real threat to the integrity of qualitative research if the priority accorded to 'insight' means that professional and technical standards are assumed to be irrelevant. Spackman, Barker and Nancarrow (2000) suggest that clients may increasingly value research that inspires, motivates and takes forward the client team, irrespective of its intrinsic veracity. They suggest that this is to be welcomed, marking a shift from researchers as technicians to researchers as knowledge-based professionals. That may be true. However, it also represents a risk to the integrity of qualitative (and quantitative) research. Recruitment practices are already a source of concern, data analysis is squeezed as clients demand overnight results, and report writing is a dying art. Why, the researcher might wonder, bother with all this expensive, difficult and time-consuming work when all the client wants is 'insight', irrespective of how this has been gained? Why not simply take the client to a bar, club or retail outlet, allow them to 'experience the consumer' in an entertaining manner, and discuss your impressions with them the next day? This could be supplemented with observations derived from magazines and television programmes about the topic. In the worst case, this practice could be established as the norm for qualitative research, with no distinction being made between an insight derived from a chance observation, and the results of a structured programme of research. In the long term, this might result in clients making poor decisions based on an incorrect understanding of the status of different data sources, and a loss of faith in the entire qualitative research industry.

In the **Insight Manager** scenario, qualitative research could become more central to the whole marketing venture. If more diverse data sources of differing reliability need to be integrated and evaluated, the trained researcher is in the best position to do this. The researcher's role could expand to include both conventional robust market research, and also a range of other ways to gain insight, including consumer contact sessions, cultural analysis, observation and ethnography. The qualitative researcher would also conduct a range of other facilitation exercises – brainstorming, sequential recycling, creative workshops – which would be understood as aimed at generating insight rather than robust data. This is similar to what Wendy Gordon describes as 'pro-search' – an innovative search for ways to uncover relevant information and insight. If conducted professionally with a clear sense of the status and meaning of these different data sources, this would be a real enhancement of the status of the researcher, or Insight Manger. He or she could co-ordinate the whole range of insight-finding activities, from large quantitative surveys, to customer contact sessions, creative workshops, group discussions and other forms of cultural analysis.

In the author's opinion, we see elements of both these scenarios in the research world today, and it is by no means clear which will dominate the future. The compressing of timescales, devaluing of analysis skills and apparent impatience among the client community with researchers who want to maintain high technical standards, do not augur well. However, scenario planning tells us nothing is inevitable, and that we can also decide which scenario we prefer and take the relevant action to make it more likely.

Qualitative researchers have the skills, experience and training to place themselves at the centre of the marketing venture. If the qualitative research industry is to make the Insight Manager scenario more likely and keep the Charlatan at bay, researchers need to:

- Develop the potential of an eclectic approach to data, methods and theory, to provide greater insight to their clients.
- Place bricolage at the centre of qualitative practice, allowing them to choose the approach most relevant to the research issue, rather than be driven by methods.
- Develop and communicate clear principles for the evaluation of different sources of data, their status and role, and ensure that the unique value of a research-based approach is understood.
- Focus their clients' attention on their analytical skills as well as their expertise in particular methods.
- Use their qualitative skills more confidently in a range of other situations to help their clients generate insight and move forwards – but ensure that clients understand the difference between these activities and more conventional, structured research.

In these ways researchers can enhance their professional status, their value to their clients and their position at the centre of the marketing enterprise – as providers of reliable data and inspiring insights.

KEY POINTS

- Qualitative researchers have developed a range of alternative methods for addressing the limitations of conventional interviewing approaches.
- In many cases, these methods are adaptations of interview-based approaches, and can be used together with more conventional approaches.

- There is little evidence of an emerging new paradigm for qualitative market research, nor is there a compelling need for a complete overhaul of qualitative methods.
- However, qualitative market researchers are broadening the range of methods, theories and data sources used. The key challenge to researchers for the future is to maintain their professional, research-based approach while integrating these divergent resources. The main changes which will influence their ability to meet this challenge are:

  o an increasing use of observational methods, both to overcome the limitations of interviewing and to address new marketing needs;
  o a move towards clients being more directly involved with consumers, and to methods that prioritise direct experience of the consumer;
  o relationships with consumers that are characterised by longer-term collaboration and partnership, rather than the more passive notion of the respondent;
  o the use of qualitative skills in a wider range of business contexts – beyond research – to facilitate innovation and creativity;
  o A move from basing research work on a single method – interviews – to a more eclectic approach. This eclecticism extends to methods, data sources and theoretical frameworks.

- If researchers downgrade their research skills and focus exclusively on providing the 'fast and dirty' results which some clients appear to demand, they risk providing misleading advice to their clients and devaluing the currency of research.
- If researchers respond to client demands for quicker, more useful and insightful data, while maintaining their professional standards and advising clients on the status of different sorts of data, they could become central to the process of Knowledge Management.

Bibliography

Adriaenssens, Charles and Cadman, Liz (1999) 'An adaptation of moderated e-mail focus groups to assess the potential for a new online (Internet) financial services offer in the UK', *Journal of the Market Research Society*, 41 (2, October): 417–24.

Alexander, Monty (1997) 'The myth at the heart of the brand: successful brands embody myths that can be analyzed', *Canadian Journal of Marketing Research*, 16: 86–94.

Alexander, Monty (2000) 'Codes and contexts: practical semiotics for the qualitative researcher', *Proceeedings of the Market Research Society Conference*. London: MRS. pp. 139–46.

Alexander, Monty and Valentine, Virginia (1989) 'Cultural class – researching the parts that social class cannot reach', *Proceedings of the Market Research Society Conference*. London: MRS. pp. 314–30.

Alexander, Monty, Burt, Max and Gower, Charlie (1995) 'Big talk, small talk. BT's strategic use of semiotics in planning its current advertising', *Proceedings of the Market Research Society Conference*. London: MRS. pp. 273–80.

Bauman, Z. (1991) *Intimations of Postmodernity*. London: Routledge.

Beasley, Ron and Chapin, Keith (1998) 'Paradoxes in cyberspace. A qualitative perspective on research through the Internet', Proceedings of ESOMAR Internet Seminar, pp. 195–200. ESOMAR.

Becatelli, Ian and Swindells, Alan (1998) 'Developing better pan-European campaigns', *Admap*, 33: 12–14.

Bloch, M. (1977) 'The past and the present in the present', *Man*, 112: 278–92.

Bloch, M. (1991) 'Language, anthropology and cognitive science', *Man*, 26: 183–98.

Booth, C. (1905) *Life and Labour of the People in London*. London: Macmillan.

Bourdieu, P. (1980) *The Logic of Practice*. Cambridge: Polity Press.

Cabinet Office (1998) *How to Consult Your Users: an Introductory Guide*. London: Cabinet Office.

Chandler, J. and Evans, F. (2000) 'Understanding impulse: the double observation method.' Paper to to AQR Observational Research Seminar. St. Neots, Cambridgeshire.

Clarke, Stella (1998) 'Lewisham Citizens' Jury 1996 – Drugs and Community Safety', in R. Sykes and A. Hedges (eds), *Panels and Juries: New Government, New Agenda*. London: Social Research Association. pp. 12–16.

Coates, Dan and Froggatt, Matthew (1998) 'On-Line qualitative research. The opportunities and limitations of conducting focus groups via the Internet', Proceedings of ESOMAR Internet Seminar, pp. 185–94.

Collier, T. (1993) 'Dynamic re-enactment', *Marketing* 5: 35–7.

Comley, Pete (2001) 'How to do … online research', in *The Research Guide to Internet Technology*. www.virtualsurveys.com/papers/howto.htm

Coote, Anna and Mattinson, Deborah (1997) *Twelve Good Neighbours: The Citizen as Juror*. London: The Fabian Society.

Damasio, A.R. (1994) *Descartes' Error: Emotion, Reason and the Human Brain*. New York: Avon Books.

Deal, Ken and Hodson, Tom (1997) 'Electronic and conventional focus groups: comparisons and relative merits', *Canadian Journal of Marketing Research*, 16: 61–71.

De Bono, E. (1992) *Serious Creativity*. London: HarperCollins.

De Chernatony, Leslie and McDonald, Malcolm (1998) *Creating Powerful Brands in Consumer, Service and Industrial Markets*. Oxford: Butterworth–Heinemann.

Deegan, Mary Jo (2001) 'The Chicago School of ethnography', in P. Atkinson, A. Coffey, S. Delamont, J. Lofland and L. Lofland (eds), *Handbook of Ethnography*. London: Sage. pp. 11–25.

Denny, Rita (1995) 'Inspiring details: the role of ethnography in a kaleidoscope age', ESOMAR Congress.

Denzin, N.K. and Lincoln, Y.S. (eds) (2000) *Handbook of Qualitative Research*, 2nd edn. London: Sage.

Desai, P. and Sills, A. (1996a) 'The contribution of research to policy making in the London Borough of Newham'. ESOMAR Conference Paper in Research for Public Policy, Budapest, 1996.

Desai, P. and Sills, A. (1996b) 'Qualitative research among ethnic minority communities in Britain', *Journal of the Market Research Society*, 38 (3, July): 247–65.

Desai, Philly and Thomas, Andrew (1998) *Public Consultation Research*. London: BMRB International and the London Borough of Hammersmith and Fulham.

Dixon, Andrew (1996) 'The vision of the future', *Proceedings of the Market Research Society Conference*. London: MRS. pp. 127–34.

Earls, Mark (2001) 'The death of marketing: what now for market research?', *Proceedings of the Market Research Society Conference*. London: MRS. pp. 331–46.

Eke, Vanessa and Comley, Pete (1999) *Moderated Email Groups: Computing Magazine Case Study*. London: Virtual Surveys.

Ereaut, Gill and Imms, Mike (2001) 'Bricolage'. Unpublished research paper.

Ereaut, Gill and Valentine, Virginia (1985) 'Who pays the piper? The sting in the tail of testimonial advertising', *Proceedings of the Market Research Society Conference*. London: MRS. pp. 127–42.

Evans-Pritchard, E. (1940) *The Nuer: A Description of the Modes of Livelihood and Political Institutions of a Nilotic People*. Oxford: Clarendon Press.

Fawcett, Jo and Laird, Andrea (2001) 'Bottoms up! Consultees' views on consultation', *Proceedings of the Market Research Society Conference*. London: MRS. pp. 297–312.

Finch, J. (1984) '"It's great to have someone to talk to": the ethics and politics of interviewing women', in *Social Researching: Politics, Problems, Practice*. London: Routledge and Kegan Paul. pp. 70–87.

Fletcher, Jonathan and Morgan, Bill (2000) 'New directions in qualitative brand research', *Proceedings of the Market Research Society Conference*. London: MRS. pp. 121–38.

Franzen, Giep and Bouwman, Margot (2001) *The Mental World of Brands: Mind, Memory and Brand Success*. Henley-on-Thames: World Advertising Research Centre.

Fuller, Kirsty and Collier, Maggie (1999) 'Choose change: forward looking research at its best'. Paper presented to Association for Qualitative Research Trends Conference.

Gatard, Christian (2001) 'The real/imaginary origins and future of qualitative research. A very subjective overview of our profession'. Association for

Qualitative Research/Qualitative Research Consultants Association Conference Proceedings, Paris.

Gibson, Rowan (1998) 'Rethinking business', in *Rethinking the Future*. London: Nicholas Brealey. pp. 1–14.

Glaros, Elizabeth (1997) 'A constructive approach to advertising testing. Shifting from the content to the form of representation in advertising'. Presentation to ESOMAR Seminar on Qualitative Research.

Gordon, Wendy (1997) *Is the Right Research Being Ill-Used? Out of the Goldfish Bowl: Can Advertising Research Ever Replicate Reality?* Henley-on-Thames: Admap.

Gordon, Wendy (1999a) *Goodthinking*. Henley-on-Thames: Admap.

Gordon, Wendy (1999b) *Researching the Future: Oxymoron or Possibility?* Henley-on-Thames: Admap.

Gordon, Wendy (2001) 'The darkroom of the mind: what does neuro-psychology now tell us about brands?' Association for Qualitative Research/Qualitative Research Consultants Association Conference Proceedings, Paris.

Gordon, W. and Langmaid, R. (1988) *Qualitative Market Research: A Practitioner's and Buyer's Guide*. Aldershot: Gower.

Gordon, Wendy and Pike, Richard (n.d.) 'Carry On Round the "U" Bend: An Experimental Comparison of Three Qualitative Methodologies'. Unpublished.

Gordon, Wendy and Valentine, Virginia (1996) 'Buying the brand at point of choice. Understanding the communication mix', *Proceedings of the Market Research Society Conference*. London: MRS. pp. 271–84.

Gormley, Richard (1995) 'The information superhighway. A new way of life for researchers', *Proceedings of the Market Research Society Conference*. London: MRS. pp. 181–200.

Hall, Kathryn (2000) 'Keeping an eye on you', *NOP News*: 3.

Hall, S. (1992) 'The question of cultural identity', in *Modernity and Its Futures*. Cambridge: Polity Press. pp. 273–326.

Harris, Cheryl (1997) 'Developing online market research methods and tools – considering theorizing interactivity: models and cases', *Marketing and Research Today* 25: 267–73.

Harvey, D. (1989) *The Condition of Post-modernity*. Oxford: Oxford University Press.

Harvey, Michael, and Evans, Malcolm (2001) 'Decoding competitive propositions: a semiotic alternative to traditional advertising research', *Proceedings of the Market Research Society Conference*. London: MRS. pp. 169–82.

Heath, Robert (2000) *Low Involvement Processing: A Neuroscientific Explanation of How Brands Work*. Henley- on-Thames: Admap.

Hedges, Alan (1974) *Testing to Destruction. A Critical Look at the Uses of Research in Advertising*. London: Institute of Practitioners in Advertising (reprinted 1998).

Hedges, Alan and Duncan, Sue (2000) 'Qualitative research in the social policy field', in *Qualitative Research in Context*. Henley-on-Thames: Admap. pp. 191–216.

Herbert, Michael (2001) 'Comparing online and face to face qualitative research: from teenagers to third agers'. Association for Qualitative Research/Qualitative Research Consultants Association Conference Proceedings, Paris.

Hirshberg, J. (1998) *The Creative Priority: Putting Innovation to Work in Your Business*. London: Penguin.

Holder, Susan and Young, David (1997) 'Researching the future in the present' ESOMAR Congress.

Humphries, David (2001) 'Consumer currency', in *AQR Directory 2001*, pp. 68–70.

Imms, Mike (2000) 'The theory of qualitative market research', in *Qualitative Research in Context*. Henley-on-Thames: Admap. pp. 1–16.

Institute for Public Policy Research/*The Guardian* (2000) *Aiming for Excellence in Public Involvement*. London: IPPR.

Jack, Fiona and Homans, Bas (2000) 'Getting closer to the consumer', ESOMAR Congress.

Jameson, F. (1991) *Postmodernism or the Cultural Logic of Late Capitalism*. London: Verso.

Johnson, Brenda and McKane, Monica (2001) 'Extending the reach of online focus groups through value added benefits: case studies'. Association for Qualitative Research/Qualitative Research Consultants Association Conference Proceedings, Paris.

Johnson, M. (1987) *The Body in the Mind: The Bodily Basics of Meaning, Imagination and Reason*. Chicago: University of Chicago Press.

Johnson, Maureen and Pinnington, Danielle (1998) 'Supporting the category management challenge: how research can contribute', *Journal of the Market Research Society*, 40 (1): 33–54.

Jones, R. (2000) *The Big Idea*. London: HarperCollins.

Klein, Naomi (2000) *No Logo*. London: HarperCollins.

Langer, Judith and Bunofsky, Terri (2001) 'Online focus groups and bulletin boards vs. in-person qualitative research: a real world comparison for *Playboy* magazine'. Association for Qualitative Research/Qualitative Research Consultants Association Conference Proceedings, Paris.

Lazar, D. (1998) 'Selected issues in the philosophy of social science', in C. Seale (ed.), *Researching Society and Culture*. London: Sage. pp. 7–22.

Leith, Alison and Riley, Nicky (1998) 'Understanding need.states and their role in developing successful marketing strategies', *Journal of the Market Research Society*, 40 (1): 25–32.

Lévi-Strauss, Claude (1962) *The Savage Mind* (English trans., 1964). Chicago: University of Chicago Press.

Lévi-Strauss, Claude (1964) *An Introduction to the Science of Mythology*, Vol. 1 (English trans., 1969). New York: Harper and Row.

Local Government Association (2000) *Enhancing Research Capacity: The Importance of Research in Modern Local Government*. London: Local Government Association.

Lovell, Neil and Henderson, Fiona (2000) 'Come together – increasing popular involvement in local decision-making', *Proceedings of the Market Research Society Conference*. London: MRS. pp. 161–80.

Malinowski, Bronislaw (1922) *Argonauts of the Western Pacific: An Account of Native Enterprise and Adventure in the Archipelagoes of Melanesian New Guinea*. London: Routledge and Kegan Paul.

Mariampolski, Hy (1997) 'Solving the problems of observational research. Field tactics in corporate ethnography', ESOMAR Congress.

Mariampolski, Hy (1999) 'The power of ethnography', *Journal of the Market Research Society*, 41 (1): 75–86.

Martin, S.J. (1998) 'Achieving best value through public engagement'. Warwick: University of Warwick/DETR Best Value Paper No. 8, Local Government Paper.

Mattimore, B.W. (1994) *99% Inspiration: Tips, Tales and Techniques for Liberating Your Business Creativity*. New York: American Management Association.

Mattinson, Deborah and Bell, Tim (2000) 'Politics and qualitative research', in *Qualitative Research in Context*. Henley-on-Thames: Admap. pp. 175–90.

Mrazek, Deborah, Dray, Susan and Dyer, Norman (1995) 'Day in the life visits. how to make them happen globally, or discovering unstated needs in a family environment', ESOMAR Congress.

Oakley, A. (1981) 'Interviewing women: a contradiction in terms', in *Doing Feminist Research*. London: Routledge. pp. 30–61.

Park, Alison (1998) 'Deliberative polling', in R. Sykes and A. Hedges (eds), *Panels and Juries: New Government, New Agenda*. London: Social Research Association.

Park, Robert E., Burgess, Ernest W. and McKenzie, Robert D. (eds) (1925) *The City*. Chicago: University of Chicago Press.

Pegram, Bill and Lee, Scott (2000) 'Observation then and now'. Presentation to AQR Observational Research Seminar. London.

Perrott, Nicky (1997) 'How Reuters is using the Web for customer surveys', *Proceedings of the Market Research Society Conference*. London: MRS. pp. 1–5.

Perrott, Nicky (2000) *A Revolution in Market Surveys*. London: MORI.

Pillot De Chenecey, Sean (2000) *The New Persuaders*. Henley-on-Thames: Admap.

Pincott, G. and Branthwaite, A. (2000) 'Nothing new under the sun', *Proceedings of the Market Research Society Conference*. London: MRS.

Pryke, Sue, Mimoni, Niki, Valentine, Virginia and Alexander, Monty (1998) 'New Labour – new culture – new consumer?', *Proceedings of the Market Research Society Conference*. London: MRS. pp. 73–84.

Renzetti, C. and Lee, R. (eds) (1993) *Researching Sensitive Topics*. London: Sage.

Richardson, Ann (1998) 'Health panels', in R. Sykes and A. Hedges (eds), *Panels and Juries: New Government, New Agenda*. London: Social Research Association. pp. 10–11.

Ringland, Gill (1998) *Scenario Planning: Managing for the Future*. Chichester: Wiley.

Rust, Langbourne (1993a) 'Observations: how to reach children in stores: marketing tactics grounded in observational research', *Journal of Advertising Research*.

Rust, Langbourne (1993b) 'Observations: parents and children shopping together: a new approach to the qualitative analysis of observational data', *Journal of Advertising Research*.

Savage, Mike (2000a) 'Direct approach', *Research Magazine*, pp. 38–9.

Savage, Mike (2000b) 'Return of Big Brother', *Research Magazine*, pp. 28–9.

Schlackman, Bill (1989) 'An historical perspective', in Sue Robson and Angela Foster (eds), *Qualitative Research in Action*. London: Edwin Arnold. pp. 15–23.

Seale, C. (ed.) (1998) *Researching Society and Culture*. London: Sage.

Silverman, D. (1993) *Interpreting Qualitative Data: Methods for Analysing Talk, Text and Interaction*. London: Sage.

Slater, D. (1998) 'Analysing cultural objects: content analysis and semiotics', in C. Seale (ed.), *Researching Society and Culture*. London: Sage. pp. 233–44.

Smith, David and Dexter, Andy (2001) 'Whenever I hear the word 'paradigm' I reach for my gun: how to stop talking and start walking', *Proceedings of the Market Research Society Conference*. London: MRS. pp. 183–218.

Spackman, Nigel, Barker, Andy and Nancarrow, Clive (2000) 'Happy New Millenium: a research paradigm for the 21st century', *Proceedings of the Market Research Society Conference*. London: MRS. pp 91–104.

Spenser, David and Wells, Stephen (2000) 'Qualitative research and innovation', in L. Marks (ed.), *Qualitative Research in Context*. Henley-on-Thames: Admap. pp. 233–52.

Stafford, Maria Royne and Stafford, Thomas F. (1993) 'Participant observation and the pursuit of truth: methodological and ethical considerations', *Journal of the Market Research Society*, 35 (1).

Stanley, Liz (2001) 'Mass-Observation's fieldwork methods', in P. Atkinson, A. Coffey, S. Delamont, J. Lofland and L. Lofland (eds), *Handbook of Ethnography*. London: Sage. pp. 92–108.

Sweet, Casey (2001) 'Lessons learned in conducting online qualitative research: Michigan State University bulletin board study'. Association for Qualitative Research/Qualitative Research Consultants Association Conference Proceedings, Paris.

Sykes, Roger and Hedges, Alan (eds) (1998) *Panels and Juries: New Government, New Agenda*. London: Social Research Association.

Thomas, Claire (2000) 'Mobile moods', *Research Magazine*, 34.

Tonkiss, Fran (1998) 'The history of the social survey', in C. Seale (ed.), *Researching Society and Culture*. London: Sage. pp. 58–71.

Trevaskis, Helen (2000) '"You had to be there". Why marketers are increasingly experiencing consumers for themselves and the impact of this on the role and remit of consumer professionals', *Proceedings of the Market Research Society Conference*. London: MRS. pp. 271–8.

Underhill, Paco (2000) *Why We Buy: The Science of Shopping*. London: Texere.

Valentine, Virginia (1995) 'Opening up the black box: switching the paradigm of qualitative research', ESOMAR Congress.

Valentine, Virginia and Gordon, Wendy (2000) 'The 21st century consumer – a new model of thinking', *Proceedings of the Market Research Society Conference*. London: MRS. pp. 77–91.

Vidich, Arthur J. and Lyman, Stanford M. (2000) 'Qualitative methods: their history in sociology and anthropology', in N. Denzin and Y. Lincoln (eds), *Handbook of Qualitative Research*, 2nd edn. London: Sage.

Walker, David (1997) 'Online research: what can and will be done?', ESOMAR Congress.

Walker, David (1998) 'Email research. A new window of opportunity?', Proceedings of ESOMAR Internet Seminar, pp. 117–33.

Walkowski, Jeff (2001) 'Online qualitative research for Motorola: lessons learned'. Association for Qualitative Research/Qualitative Research Consultants Association Conference Proceedings, Paris.

Walsh, D. (1998) 'Doing ethnography', in C. Seale (ed.), *Researching Society and Culture*. London: Sage. pp. 217–32.

Walter, Peter and Donaldson, Stephen (2000) '"Seeing Is believing". Consumers do not live in reports and charts, so why is consumer insight so often communicated in that way?', *Proceedings of the Market Research Society Conference*. London: MRS. pp. 59–64.

Wellcome Trust (1998) *Public Perspectives on Human Cloning*. London: Wellcome Trust.

White, Clarissa, Lewis, Jane and Elam, Gillian (1998) *Citizens' Juries: an Appraisal of Their Role Based on the Conduct of Two Women Only Juries*. London: Cabinet Office.

White, Tracey, Redfern, Sue and Maitland, Jennie (1997) 'Alternative qualitative methodologies: are we developing them just for the hell of it?', ESOMAR Congress.

Woods, Richard (1999) 'Can consumers tell you what they want?', *Market Leader*.

Index